W9-AHH-905

FOLLOWING THE COMEDY TRAIL

FOLLOWING THE COMEDY TRAIL

A GUIDE TO LAUREL AND HARDY
AND OUR GANG FILM LOCATIONS

By Leon Smith

POMEGRANATE PRESS, LTD. LOS ANGELES • LONDON

This is a Pomegranate Press, Ltd. Book

An updated compilation of A GUIDE TO LAUREL AND HARDY MOVIE LOCATIONS (1982)
and FOLLOWING THE COMEDY TRAIL (1984)
Text copyright © 1982, 1984, 1988 by Leon Smith
All contemporary photographs are by the author unless otherwise credited.
Photographs © 1982, 1984, 1988 by Leon Smith.

Published By Pomegranate Press, Ltd.
First Printing 1988

All rights reserved. No part of this book may be reproduced or transmitted in any form or by any means,
electronic or mechanical, including photocopying, recording, or by any information storage and retrieval system
without written permission from the author, except for the inclusion of brief quotes in a review.

The Library of Congress Catalog Card Number is 88-061063
ISBN 0-938817-05-1

A Note on the composition:
Cover Design: Tony Gleeson
Book Design: Ben Martin
Xerox Ventura Publisher ® Consultant: Leroy Chen
Editorial Assistant: Kathleen Resch
Cover Photograph Hand Colored By Jean Pritchard
Typesetting and page formatting by computer using
Xerox Ventura Publisher ® and Microsoft Word ® software
output through an NEC LC890 Postscript ® PagePrinter.
Body type set in ITC Bookman
Head type set in Friz Quadrata
Printed and Bound in the United States of America
by McNaughton and Gunn, Inc. of Ann Arbor, Michigan

Pomegranate Press, Ltd.
3236 Bennett Drive
Los Angeles, California 90068

FOLLOWING THE COMEDY TRAIL
An updated compilation of the Author's
A GUIDE TO LAUREL AND HARDY MOVIE LOCATIONS (1982)
and
FOLLOWING THE COMEDY TRAIL (1984)

By the same author

A GUIDE TO LAUREL AND HARDY MOVIE LOCATIONS (1982)

FOLLOWING THE COMEDY TRAIL (1984)

HOLLYWOOD GOES ON LOCATION (1988)

The Thomas Bros. Map references listed throughout this text refer to coordinates in the current edition of The Thomas Guide, Los Angeles/Orange County Street Atlas and Directory, which are on sale at most Los Angeles stationery and book stores, or can be ordered by mail from:

Thomas Bros. Maps and Books
603 West Seventh Street
Los Angeles, CA 90017
Telephone (213) 627 4018

ACKNOWLEDGEMENTS

Acknowledgements are definitely in order for the following very special people and organizations without whose assistance this publication could not have been completed.

Bessie Freiden of The Culver City Historical Society;

Robert Cushman, Carol Cullen, Carol Epstein, and Michele McCauley of The Academy of Motion Picture Arts and Sciences;

Bill Hogue of the M-G-M Studios;

Leith Adams of the USC-Warner Bros. Film Archives;

Cathy and Eric King of Photoking Labs, Hollywood

Bob Bonday

Smae Spaulding Davis

Marcy Robin

Perry Shields

Georgia Smith

Katherine Smith

Jim Walters

Very special thanks to Rob Word of the Hal Roach Studios for permission to use the Laurel and Hardy and Our Gang photographs. Photographs courtesy of Hal Roach Studios Inc. Copyright© owned by Hal Roach Studios, Inc.

For Georgia and Katherine Marie and to the men, women, boys and girls of the motion picture industry who worked so hard to make millions of people around the world laugh and laugh and laugh.

Author Leon Smith on the famous MUSIC BOX stairs.

Detective Leon Smith, a 30-year veteran of the Los Angeles Police Department, guides us on a nostalgic journey to famous Laurel and Hardy and Our Gang movie locations. His investigations reveal exact addresses of these historical sites and feature his present-day photographs along with many production stills showing how the locations appeared in the original film.

A life-long movie buff with a special interest in discovering and photographing Los Angeles film locations, Leon Smith is a writer, photographer, and film and book critic.

Walk in the footsteps of Laurel and Hardy and Our Gang. Visit POTTSVILLE. Join Our Gang GOIN' FISHIN'. Climb THE MUSIC BOX stairs.

How does Smith verify his sites? "I count layers of bricks and sets of windows and then match them to the buildings in old production stills, or talk to old-timers who were present during the filming. Sometimes as I'm driving along I see a view – hills, railway tracks, a church spire – that matches up perfectly with a scene I remember in a movie. A lot of it is just leg work...good old police procedure...and digging through old Spanish land grant maps at the Bureau of Engineering.".

To confirm the authenticity of each site, Smith has personally visited all locations included in this book. And he provides the address of each location to benefit those fans who may also plan a visit.

AUTHOR'S NOTES

Going to a house in a secluded, quiet neighborhood or to a building in a busy commercial area just to take a photograph would be, to the "normal" person, pure folly. But to an ardent fan of Laurel and Hardy and Our Gang, if that house or building is an authentic location appearing in one of these Hal Roach classic comedies—well, it becomes a shrine. So, with camera in hand, here are some shrines for those who care.

BEFORE YOU BEGIN

Some of the commercial property and buildings you will see are public. But those that are residences are, of course, private. Use discretion and courtesy when visiting any locations and do not trespass on private property.

FILM SITE VERIFICATIONS

All movie sites have been identified through reviews of films, still photographs taken at the time of filming, printed matter relating to the films, and interviews with persons who were present at locations during the production of the films. Many structures are virtually the same today as they appeared in the films; others over the years have been architecturally altered significantly.

CONTENTS

PREFACE

Hollywood, California, doesn't exist. It's a zip code for an area a few miles northwest of downtown Los Angeles.

The "Hollywood" of Laurel and Hardy and Our Gang was mostly Culver City—a small community virtually surrounded by the western section of Los Angeles: the home of Hal Roach Studios and its neighbor, M-G-M. Fortunately for film buffs, many scenes were shot in the same area but outside the studios. Other locations were in West Los Angeles and downtown Los Angeles.

"Progress" has erased many of these film sites, but years ago I decided to visit those that remained. I began with the famous Laurel and Hardy MUSIC BOX stairs. The authentic location, I was assured, was on Silver Lake Blvd. overlooking the west side of the lake. I spent the better part of a morning examining every square inch of the area. No trace of the stairs. Further research suggested they were at the east side of the lake and that their bottom third was now missing because of road construction. Sure enough, at the end of Cove Street, just east of Silver Lake Blvd., I finally found stairs. I didn't care a bit that the lowest third was gone. I was there!

I did notice that these stairs did not look exactly as they had in the film; for one thing, they were much wider. However, I made a return trip with my camera and my son just to have my photograph taken where (as I then thought) the Boys had stood. Months later I was both shocked and pleased when I read in a trade paper that the MUSIC BOX stairs were at Vendome Street and Del Monte Drive, a few miles south of Silver Lake. The next day I hurried to that intersection and, lo and behold, there they were! The correct width and the bottom third intact, just as I remembered them. I was *really* there!

Deciding never again to depend on hearsay information, I embarked upon a crusade of sorts: to find Laurel and Hardy and Our Gang loca-tions and to authenticate them, not only by pinpointing existing landmarks but by interviewing the few remaining dedicated people who worked on and in the films. Without their verification, existing locations could become an invisible part of film history.

Over the years, I have visited and confirmed many of the Laurel and Hardy and Our Gang locations. The photographs and maps in this book are those that I first compiled for my own use—and that I am sharing with other fans as a guide to those precious locations—to offer my fellow film buffs the opportunity of knowing that they, too, are really there!

THE CULVER CITY AREA

WHERE IT ALL BEGAN

DIRECTIONS

Many Culver City streets angle and are not in a true north, south, east or west direction. So, to avoid confusion to those not familiar with the area, I've given all directions to film sites as either north, south, east or west instead of northwest, southeast, etc.

Where to begin? I suggest where it all began on Washington Boulevard. At the time of demolition, the address of the Hal Roach Studios was 8822 Washington Boulevard. Many Culver City streets, however, were renumbered in the 1930s. The correct address of the studio during the early golden days of comedy was 6718 Washington Boulevard.

Exit the Santa Monica Freeway (10) or the San Diego Freeway (405) at Washington Boulevard. Go to National Boulevard. The Hal Roach Studio site (now an automobile agency) is at 8822 Washington Boulevard (1). The plaque commemorating the studio's contribution to motion picture comedy is located east of the automobile agency (across the railroad tracks) in a very small but charming park (2) on the southwest corner of the intersection. Go east on Washington Boulevard to Caroline Avenue. Turn right (south) and go to Jacob Street. The house seen in *BIG BUSINESS* (3) is located on the southeast corner. The address is 3403/3406 Caroline Avenue. This was the "first" stop Laurel and Hardy made in the film. Return to Washington Boulevard and National Boulevard. Go south on National Boulevard to Helms Avenue. Turn right (west). The

house seen in the final scene of the Our Gang film *DOGS IS DOGS* is located at 3584 (4). Return to Washington Boulevard. Turn left (west) and go to Van Buren Place. Turn left (south). The building (5) located at 3916 was seen in the Laurel and Hardy *WE FAW DOWN*. Across Washington Boulevard from this site is the Adams Hotel (6). Its address is 3896 Main Street, Culver City. The Culver Boulevard side of the hotel was seen in Laurel and Hardy's *WE FAW DOWN*. The alley behind the building was seen in their film *LIBERTY*. The front of the hotel was also seen in *LIBERTY* as actress Jean Harlow and escort were about to enter a taxi.

Directly across Main Street from the Adams Hotel's entrance is the famous Culver City Hotel, the "pie-shaped" building (7) seen in Laurel & Hardy's *PUTTING PANTS ON PHILIP*. The address of the building is 9501 Culver Boulevard, Culver City. The film site (the entrance to the building) is on Main Street.

Across Culver Boulevard from the Culver City Hotel, on the west side of Main Street, is the building (8) seen in the background during the traffic jam scene in Laurel and Hardy's *LEAVE 'EM LAUGHING*. A little farther north, toward Venice Boulevard, is (9) the building seen in the Laurel and Hardy film *TWO TARS*. Its address is 3815 Main Street, Culver City. The buildings across the street, on the east side of Main Street and north of Culver Boulevard (10), were also seen in the film. Farther north, Main Street intersects with Venice Boulevard.

At this point, Culver City ends and Los Angeles begins. Main Street becomes Bagley Avenue. The building on the northeast corner (11) was seen in the final scenes of Laurel and Hardy's *HATS OFF*. The building on the opposite corner (the northwest corner) (12) was also seen in the film as was Bagley Avenue. Both buildings and Bagley Avenue were also seen in their film *BACON GRABBERS* as they roared down Venice Boulevard in their Model T and turned on Bagley Avenue enroute to Cheviot Hills and a meeting with Edgar Kennedy.

Go east on Venice Boulevard to Helms Avenue. Make a "U" turn at the intersection. Go west on Venice Boulevard to Vera Avenue. Turn right on Vera Avenue (north). Go to 3120 (13) the house seen in Laurel and Hardy's *PERFECT DAY*. The house next door (north) (14) was the house of the neighbor who was seen watering the lawn as the Boys and their entourage entered their car to begin a trip to a picnic. The address is 3116. The garage behind the house has a very distinctive double gable. Their building was soon often in the film. Across the street, 3115 (15) is the house seen in the film with neighbors sitting in the front yard waving and calling "Good-bye!" each time the Boys entered their Model T.

Return to Venice Boulevard. Turn right (west) and go to Culver Boulevard. Turn left and continue to Main Street. Turn left (south) and go to Washington Boulevard. Main Street ends here and Van Buren Place begins. Continue south on Van Buren Place to Farragut Drive. Turn right (west) and go to 9634. This is the house (16) seen in Our Gang's *CANNED FISHING*. The row of garages and the alley seen in the closing segment of the film are adjacent to the house. Continue west on Farragut Drive to Lafayette Place. Turn right (north) on Lafayette Place and go to 4052. The group of houses on the east side of the street (17) were seen in the Our Gang film *SMALL TALK*. Return to Culver Boulevard. Turn left (west) and go to 9760 (18), the famous Fire Department Number 1. This building was seen in the same Our Gang film. The street immediately west of this site is Duquesne Avenue. The Culver City City Hall is on the southeast corner. Its address is 9970 Culver Boulevard (19). This building was the site of Laurel and Hardy's *COUNTY HOSPITAL* in 1932 and *GOING BYE-BYE!* in 1934. Near the northwest corner of the intersection is the *site* of the apartment building (20) seen in both of these films. The massive M-G-M building now occupies this site.

Continue west on Culver Boulevard to Madison Avenue. Turn left (south) and go to 4175 (21), the *site* of the house seen in the Laurel and Hardy film *HOG WILD*. The garage seen in this film is at the back of the lot. The house next door seen in the film was located at 4171 (22). I say *was* as the house was recently demolished and another house occupies the site. The famous duplex (23) seen in the film is on the opposite side of the house at 4175. Its address is 4181. The landmark house (24) seen throughout the opening scenes of the film is located across the street at 4170. Another structure prominent in the film is located on La Salle Avenue, the street immediately west of Madison Avenue. Its address is 4148 (25).

Return to Culver Boulevard. Turn right (east) and go to Madison Avenue. Turn left (north). At the intersection of Grant Avenue is the entrance to M-G-M (now Lorimar) Studios parking area. The classic entrance to the studio so familiar to motion picture fans around the world is just around the corner on Washington Boulevard. In the studio complex is the famous school (26) so many of the M-G-M child actors attended, including many members of Our Gang. The structure is now named "The Joan Crawford Building". Permission *MUST* be obtained to visit this studio.

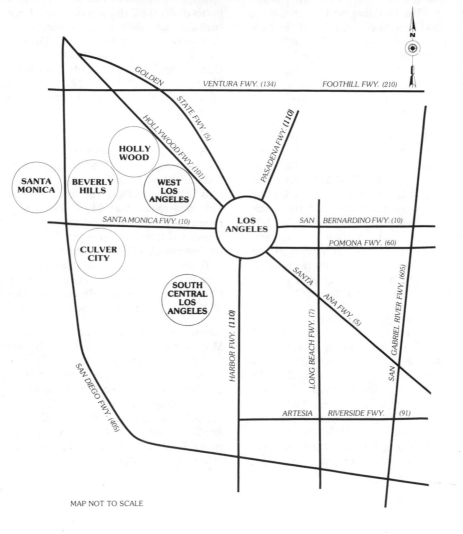

MAP NOT TO SCALE

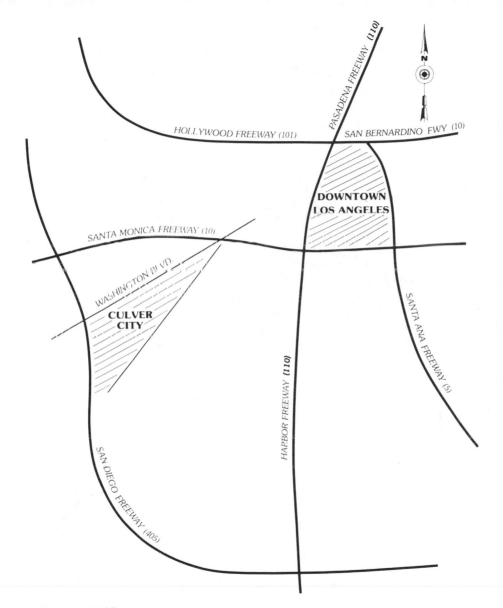

N

HOLLYWOOD FREEWAY (101)

SAN BERNARDINO FWY (10)

PASADENA FREEWAY (110)

DOWNTOWN
LOS ANGELES

SANTA MONICA FREEWAY (10)

WASHINGTON BLVD.

CULVER
CITY

SANTA ANA FREEWAY (5)

HARBOR FREEWAY (110)

SAN DIEGO FREEWAY (405)

MAP NOT TO SCALE

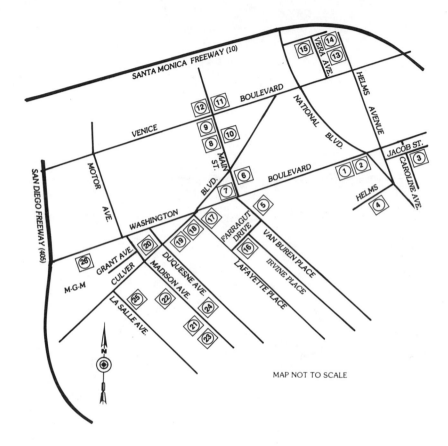

MAP NOT TO SCALE

WHERE IT ALL BEGAN

BRUCE TORRENCE HOLLYWOOD HISTORICAL COLLECTION.

Aerial photograph of Hal Roach Studios in 1934.

HAL ROACH STUDIOS

Site of Hal Roach Studios, 8822 Washington Boulevard,
Culver City.

The photograph on page 20 was taken in 1934, the year the Hal Roach Studio was at the height of its popularity. During this year the studio released Laurel and Hardy's SONS OF THE DESERT, THE PRIVATE LIFE OF OLIVER THE EIGHTH, THEM THAR HILLS, BABES IN TOYLAND, THE LIVE GHOST and GOING BYE-BYE! and Our Gang's HI-NEIGHBOR!, FOR PETE'S SAKE!, THE FIRST ROUND-UP, HONKEY DONKEY, MIKE FRIGHT, WASHEE IRONEE, MAMA'S LITTLE PIRATE, and SHRIMPS FOR A DAY.

As a note of interest, Lake Laurel and Hardy can be seen behind the administration building in this photograph. This lake was seen in BABES IN TOYLAND. The administration building was utilized as part of the lumber mill in the Boys' BUSY BODIES in 1933.

Thomas Bros. Map Reference: Page 42 at D5.

WHERE IT ALL BEGAN

(ALMOST)

A marker is located in a small park at the southwest corner of Washington Boulevard and National Boulevard, Culver City.

As appropriate and appreciated as this marker is to Laurel and Hardy fans throughout the world, the small park is not the site of the world famous Hal Roach Studios. The actual location of the studio complex is west of the railroad tracks that border the west side of the park, approximately 50 yards from the location of the marker.

Thomas Bros. Map reference: Page 42 at D 5.

Laurel and Hardy in car with Christmas trees.

BIG BUSINESS

Jacob Street near Caroline Avenue.

THE PLAYERS

Stanley Laurel
James Finlayson

Stanley Sandford

Oliver Hardy
Lyle Tayo

Released April 20, 1929 by M-G-M

3404/3406 Caroline Avenue, Culver City.

Selling Christmas trees in July? That's the very odd goal of Laurel and Hardy in this film. And to prove they can sell the trees, they decide to demonstrate their salesmanship to homeowner James Finlayson after being rather violently turned down by their first prospective customer, Lyle Tayo. The end result is the destruction of both Finlayson's home and Laurel and Hardy's car.

The location of the first stop is a duplex now at 3404/3406 Caroline Avenue in Culver City. The "long street" Laurel & Hardy drove down and parked on is Jacob Street. Even though a fence has been installed around the side yard of the house facing Jacob Street, all windows and doors, especially the distinctive canopy over the door with its tile roof and arched supports, appear today as they did in the film.

The front porch of the duplex is the primary film location. This is where the Boys made their first two stops. The door on the left (3404) is the one where Lyle Tayo met and talked with them. The right-hand door (3406) is the one where a woman's arm appears, a hammer firmly clutched in her hand (probably Lyle Tayo again), and bops Ollie in the head. See Page 103 for another location of this film.

Thomas Bros. Map reference: Page 42 at D 5.

DOGS IS DOGS

3584 Helms Avenue, Culver City.

THE PLAYERS

Bobby "Wheezer" Hutchins
Sherwood "Spud" Bailey
Billy Gilbert

Matthew "Stymie" Beard
Dorothy De Borba
Pete the Pup

Released November 21, 1931 by M-G-M

Our Gang's Wheezer (Bobby Hutchins) and Dorothy (Dorothy De Borba) live with their stepmother (Blanche Payson), convinced that their long-absent father has forgotten about them. After the usual Our Gang antics, Wheezer, Dorothy and even Pete the Pup (who has ended up in the dog pound) are "rescued" by their aunt (Lyle Tayo) and taken to their father who has been "very ill and unable to come for them."

The house seen in the closing scene is located at 3584 Helms Avenue, Culver City.

An eyewitness present during filming verified this location for me. Although the house has been significantly remodeled (its porch, for example, is now enclosed) the line of the roof is very similar to that in the film. The Baldwin Hills seen in the distance line up with the 1931 camera angles.

Thomas Bros. Map reference: Page 42 at D 6.

A fast exit from the Adams Hotel.

WE FAW DOWN

The Culver Boulevard side of the Adams Hotel.

THE PLAYERS

Stanley Laurel
George Kotsonaros
Kay Deslys

Bess Flowers
Vera White

Oliver Hardy
Vivien Oakland
Allen Cavan

Released December 29, 1928 by M-G-M

Laurel and Hardy, out on the town without their wives, come to the aid of two ladies when one of the women loses her hat in a gust of wind. In trying to retrieve it, Stan and Ollie fall into a mud puddle. The ladies invite the boys to their nearby apartment and offer to clean and dry their soiled clothing. The Boys' wives learn of their husbands' whereabouts and raid the apartment, shotguns in hand. An edited version of this scene was used ten years later for the closing moments of BLOCK-HEADS (1938).

The apartment building where Laurel and Hardy "undressed" is the

The Adams Hotel as seen from across Culver Boulevard.

3916 Van Buren Place, Culver City.

Adams Hotel, 3896 Main Street. The side seen in the film faces Culver Boulevard.

Stan and Ollie fell into the mud puddle in front of a building at 3916 Van Buren Place, just around the corner from the Adams Hotel.

The side of the Adams Hotel seen in the film is unchanged since 1928. The two sets of double windows and the small window to their right can be identified six decades later by the tapered wooden decorations of the window frames.

The curb and drain in front of the mud-puddle building are as they appeared in the film; the building itself has been remodeled.

Thomas Bros. Map reference: Page 42 at C 6.

In the gutter on the east side of Van Buren Place.

Changing trousers in the alley in 1929.

LIBERTY

The alley beside the Adams Hotel, 3896 Main Street,
Culver City.

THE PLAYERS

Stanley Laurel		Oliver Hardy
James Finlayson	Tom Kennedy	Harlean Carpenter*
Harry Bernard	Ed Brandenberg	Sam Lufkin
Jack Raymond	Jack Hill	*(Jean Harlow)

Released January 26, 1929 by M-G-M

Adams Hotel in 1982.

Adams Hotel in 1987.

Laurel and Hardy, assisted by friends on the outside with a fast car, escape from jail. In their haste to change from prison garb into street clothing in the back seat of the car, they quickly discover they have each other's trousers on.

Dumped by their friends, Laurel and Hardy hide behind a building and attempt to exchange the trousers. An alert policeman pursues them down an alley. The Boys ditch the policeman, then find a hiding place in a taxi. They are safe there until a beautiful young lady (Jean Harlow) and her escort exit the Adams Hotel and attempt to enter the taxi. The se- quence immediately following was shot in downtown Los Angeles; see Page 132.

The building in both scenes was the Adams Hotel, 3986 Main Street, Culver City. The trouser exchange was filmed in the alley on the east side of the building, the taxi scene at its

9430 Washington Boulevard, Culver City.

In front of the Adams Hotel as Jean Harlow prepares to enter a taxi. Note the same windows in the building in the background.

entrance. The building in the back-ground is across the street from the Adams Hotel at 9430 Washington Boulevard.

Particular attention was given to authenticating this site because the Adams Hotel has been altered some-what over the years and is now being demolished. You will notice, for ex-ample, that the small window in the alley photograph has been lengthened, and the air vent below the window filled and plastered over. Using enlarged photographs—stills from the time of filming and those that I had taken recently—I counted the rows of bricks and identified con-struction marks as well as several "scars of time". I am convinced that this alley is the location used in the film.

Thomas Bros. Map reference: Page 42 at C 6.

PUTTING PANTS ON PHILIP

THE PLAYERS

Stanley Laurel
Sam Lufkin
Ed Brandbenberg

Oliver Hardy
Harvey Clark
Dorothy Coburn

Released December 3, 1927 by M-G-M

9501 Culver Boulevard, Culver City, as it is today.

Hardy goes to the dock to meet Laurel, who is arriving by boat from Scotland—and is appalled to see his friend in kilts. Hardy tries and fails to disassociate himself from the strange visitor. After evading many curious females who want a closer look at the man in a "skirt", Ollie leads Stan to a tailor's shop

In front of the "Harry H. Culver and Company" building.

A view of the film site from across Main Street.

where he is measured for trousers.

Much of this film was shot on Main Street, near Culver Boulevard in Culver City. One scene was filmed in front of the Culver City Hotel at 9501 Culver Boulevard. The entryway seen in the film is actually on Main Street facing the Adams Hotel.

The Main Street entrance to the building has been modified and made smaller; note the pattern of stonework, especially the corner on the right side of the door. Also note

Detail of the front of the building today.

the four small holes in each stone column, the location of the signs seen in the film.

The bank of windows on the left side of the doorway are unchanged since 1927 except for temporary boards covering the lower half.

Thomas Bros. Map reference: Page 42 at C 6.

Main Street traffic jam in Culver City.

LEAVE 'EM LAUGHING

3839 Main Street, Culver City. Note the distinctive
three-tiered cap along the top of the building.

THE PLAYERS

Stanley Laurel	Oliver Hardy
Edgar Kennedy	Charlie Hall
Viola Richard	Dorothy Coburn
Stanley Sandford	Sam Lufkin
Edgar Dearing	Al Hallet
Jack Lloyd	Otto Fries

Jack Hill

Released January 28, 1928 by M-G-M

After a visit to their dentist, Laurel and Hardy find that driving and laughing gas are a bad mix. Their erratic driving and hysterical laughter results in an enormous traffic jam that does not amuse traffic cop Edgar Kennedy.

The most prominent building in the film—3839 Main Street in Culver City—is now occupied by an office supply company. The Culver City department store was demolished and a Bank of America building now stands on the site.

Please note the distinctive 3-edged cap running along the top of the building, which is evident in the still photographs taken during filming.

Thomas Bros. Map reference: Page 42 at C 6.

TWO TARS

A messy Main Street sidewalk.

THE PLAYERS

Stanley Laurel   Oliver Hardy   Thelma Hill
Ruby Blaine   Edgar Kennedy   Charlie Hall

Released November 3, 1928 by M-G-M

3815 S. Main Street, Culver City.

Assuming the roles of sailors, Laurel and Hardy rent a car, pick up two girls and head for a drive in the country. A traffic jam leads to short tempers, then to the destruction of virtually every car on the highway. (The following scene was shot at another location; see Page 117.

Laurel and Hardy pick up the girls on Main Street in Culver City. The buildings in the photograph are on the east side of Main Street at the corner of Culver Boulevard; they were in the background of the opening scenes. I photographed the original façade of the building shortly after the metal facing was removed during remodeling. An accompanying photograph shows the buildings as they appear today.

Thomas Bros. Map reference: Page 42 at C 6.

Northeast corner of Main Street and Culver Boulevard, Culver City, during remodeling.

Northeast corner of Main Street and Culver Boulevard today.

The famous hat fight scene in the middle.
of Venice Boulevard.

HATS OFF

9401 and 9349 Venice Boulevard, Los Angeles.

THE PLAYERS

Stanley Laurel   Oliver Hardy   James Finlayson

Anita Gavin   Sam Lufkin   Dorothy Coburn

Released November 5, 1927 by M-G-M

Handymen Laurel and Hardy try to deliver a large washing machine to a house at the top of a long flight of cement stairs. After many attempts to struggle up the steps, they end up in the middle of an intersection engaged in a fight with irate pedestrians who virtually destroy one another's hats.

The famous hat-fight scene was shot at the intersection of Venice Boulevard and Bagley Avenue in West Los Angeles. (Many earlier sequences were filmed in the Silver Lake area; see page 152).

Thomas Bros. Map reference: Page 342 at C 6.

9349 Venice Boulevard, Los Angeles, looking
north on Bagley Avenue.

BACON GRABBERS

9349 Venice Boulevard, Los Angeles.

THE PLAYERS

Stanley Laurel
Jean Harlow

Oliver Hardy
Charlie Hall

Edgar Kennedy
Bobby Dunn

Released October 19, 1929, by M-G-M

Now on the right side of the law, process servers Laurel and Hardy are looking for Edgar Kennedy, who has not paid for his radio. In an opening scene, they guide their Model T down Bagley Avenue from Venice Boulevard toward the fashionable Cheviot Hills. The drive begins at 9349 Venice Boulevard. (See page 99 for the Cheviot Hills location.)

Thomas Bros. Map reference: Page 42 at C 6.

PERFECT DAY

THE PLAYERS

Stanley Laurel
Edgar Kennedy
Harry Bernard
Lyle Tayo

Kay Deslys
Clara Guiol

Oliver Hardy
Isabelle Keith
Baldwin Cooke
Charley Rogers

Released August 10, 1929 by M-G-M

3120 Vera Avenue, Los Angeles.

Laurel and Hardy's wives (Kay Deslys and Isabelle Keith) plan a family picnic on a sunny Sunday. A cranky uncle with gout (Edgar Kennedy), a flat tire and assorted neighbors delay the trip. Finally, Laurel and Hardy, their wives and uncle get things in order, then drive down the street and straight into a construction zone where the car and all therein sink in a deep mudhole. The house used in this film as the

In the car in front of the house at 3120 Vera Avenue.

3115 Vera Avenue, Los Angeles.

3116 Vera Avenue, Los Angeles, in 1980.

home of Laurel and Hardy is located at 3120 Vera Avenue, Los Angeles. It has changed little over the years. At the house across the street (3115 Vera Avenue), neighbors Henry Bernard and Clara Guiol waved and called "Good-bye!" The next-door house (3116 Vera Avenue) is where neighbor Baldwin Cooke waters his lawn and later, in a heated argument, throws a brick through the windshield of the Boys' car. Although greatly remoded, the house at 3116 is the same one seen in the film. The photograph (above right) shows the garage at the rear of the house with the double gable. This structure was very evident in the film.

Thomas Bros. Map reference: Page 42 at D 5.

3116 Vera Avenue today. Note the recently built addition.

Our Gang members in back yard of "Spanky's" house
next to the long wall.

CANNED FISHING

THE PLAYERS

George "Spanky" McFarland
Billie "Buckwheat" Thomas
Gary "Junior" Jasgar

Carl "Alfalfa" Switzer
Eugene "Porky" Lee

Released February 12, 1938 by M-G-M

"Spanky's" house and the wall as it is today.

This site appeared throughout this Our Gang film and was used as part of an opening logo for the television series THE LITTLE RASCALS, shown in the Los Angeles area for many years.

The Culver City neighborhood has changed little since 1938. The low wall still stands, as it appeared in the film, separating George . "Spanky" McFarland's house from an alley.

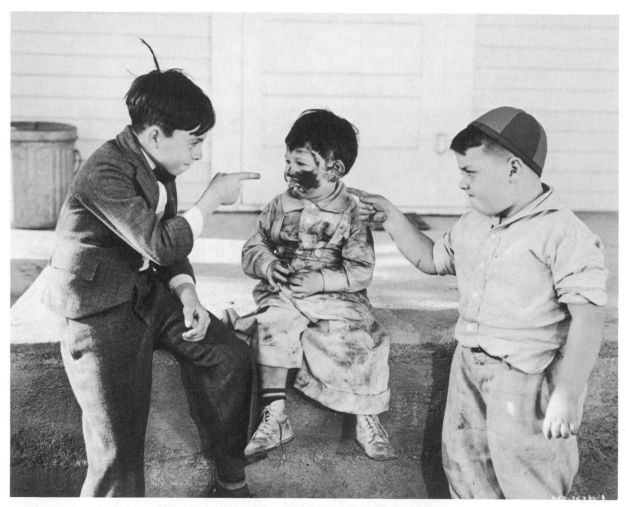

"Alfalfa" Switzer, Gary Jasgar and "Spanky" McFarland.
on the back porch of "Spanky's" house.

The garage across the alley from "Spanky's" house.

Across the alley is the big wooden garage with a series of double doors, also seen in the film. "Spanky's" back porch, a cement slab in 1938, is visible. The alley leading toward distant Baldwin Hills is now thick with foliage and barely resembles the avenue of escape the Gang took in the closing scene of the film.

"Spanky's" house is located at 9634 Farragut Drive, between Irvine Place and Lafayette Place in Culver City.

Thomas Bros. Map reference: Page 42 at C 6.

The alley Our Gang ran down in the final scene of the film.

SMALL TALK

THE PLAYERS

Bobby "Wheezer" Hutchins
Mary Ann Jackson

Joe Cobb
Allen "Farina" Hoskins

Jean Darling
Pete the Pup

Released May 18, 1929, by M-G-M

4052 Lafayette Place, Culver City.

Members of Our Gang portray orphans who desperately want parents. "Wheezer" (Bobby Hutchins) is adopted and taken to a beautiful home, where the rest of the Gang pay him an unscheduled visit. Mary Ann Jackson and Jean Darling accidentally set off a fire and police alarm, creating chaos for Wheezer

9760 Culver Boulevard, Culver City.
(Fire Department Number 1)

Culver Boulevard, Culver City.

and his new parents.

The interiors of Wheezer's new home were shot in the studio. The location where fire and police vehicles arrived was at 4052 Lafayette Place. Note the row of houses with prominent chimneys facing the street which are very evident in the film. The fire and police cars began their trek to Wheezer's house at Fire Department Number 1, a real fire station at 9760 Culver Boulevard. The Culver City City Hall is the building next door. In the distance is the famous Culver City Hotel, a building seen many times in Laurel and Hardy and Our Gang films.

Thomas Bros. Map reference: Page 42 at C 6.

The front entrance to the Culver City City Hall - the
entrance to a hospital in COUNTY HOSPITAL and the
entrance to a court in GOING BYE-BYE!

COUNTY HOSPITAL

City Hall from same angle as seen on opposite page.

THE PLAYERS

Stanley Laurel	Oliver Hardy	Billy Gilbert
Sam Lufkin	Baldwin Cooke	Ham Kinsey
May Wallace	Frank Holliday	Lilyan Irene
Belle Hare	Dorothy Layton	William Austin

Released June 25, 1932 by M-G-M

Hardy is recuperating in "County Hospital"—actually Culver City's City Hall at 9770 Culver Boulevard. All goes well until Laurel pays a visit. He causes so many problems that Ollie's doctor (Billy Gilbert) discharges his patient early. Stan, unaware that he sat down on a soporific-filled hypodermic needle, offers to drive his buddy home. The drive ends in a spectacular collision with a streetcar (see page 123).

The photographs of Culver Boulevard in front of the City Hall show the camera angle used when the Boys were "kicked out" of the hospital. The apartment building across the street is at 9939 Culver Boulevard.

Thomas Bros. Map reference: Page 42 at C 6.

Culver City City Hall.

Intersection of Culver Boulevard and Duquesne Avenue.
In front of the City Hall.

Apartment building (before demolition) seen in film.
9939 Culver Boulevard.

GOING BYE-BYE!

Culver City City Hall, 9770 Culver Boulevard.

THE PLAYERS

Stanley Laurel	Oliver Hardy
Walter Long	Mae Busch
Sam Lufkin	Harry Dunkinson
Elinor Van Der Veer	Baldwin Cooke
Fred Holmes	Jack Lipson
Lester Dorr	Charles Dorety

Released June 23, 1934 by M-G-M

On the right side of the law again, concerned citizens Laurel and Hardy testify against a killer (Walter Long). He is sentenced to life in the state prison, and swears to "break out and get even." Laurel and Hardy agree to leave town. They decide to take along a traveling companion to share expenses. Their choice—ironically—is Long's girl friend (Mae Busch). Before the journey begins, Long effects his escape and finds Laurel and Hardy in Busch's apartment. And revenge is his!

The Culver City Hall was used again, this time as a court building in the opening scenes of this film. The photograph shows the cement light pole next to the mailbox and the distant light pole with the decorative standards beneath its two globes. Both poles remain virtually unchanged today. The apartment building across Culver Boulevard at 9939 (also seen in COUN- TY HOSPITAL) was demolished. The M- G-M office building, the Filmland Corporate Center, now occupies the site.

Thomas Bros. Map reference: Page 42 at C 6.

The intersection of Duquesne Avenue and Culver Boulevard, Culver City.

Apartment building at 9939
Culver Boulevard,
Culver City.

Apartment building site in 1984.

Apartment building site today - the Filmland Corporate
Center building, new home of Metro-Goldwyn-Mayer studios.

Laurel and Hardy attempting to put up a radio antenna.
Photo shows garage at rear of driveway as it was in the film

HOG WILD

THE PLAYERS

Stanley Laurel   Oliver Hardy

Fay Holderness   Dorothy Granger

Charles McMurphy

Released May 31, 1930 by M-G-M

4175 Madison Avenue, Culver City.

Ollie's wife (Fay Holderness) wants a radio antenna on the roof of their house. While Hardy is installing it, Laurel drops by and gives a hand. The ensuing chaos continues as the Boys careen through the streets of Culver City and culminates when their Model T collides with a streetcar. (See page 127 for accident location.)

The house often identified as the Hardys' is at 4175 Madison Avenue, Culver City, at the back of the lot. It was, supposedly, moved from its original position at the front of the

At left, 4177 Madison Avenue, Culver City.

Below, 4171 Madison Avenue, Culver City in 1984.

property, 4177 Madison, now occupied by another house. I carefully inspected the house, with the permission of its owner, and found no structural similarity to the house used in the film. My guess is that the original house was demolished. The garage, however, remains. But not in the position used in filming: it *has* been moved to the back of the lot.

At left, 4171 Madison Avenue today.

At right, 4181 Madison Avenue, Culver City.

Below, 4170 Madison Avenue, Culver City

Other nearby structures seen often in the film include (next door on either side) an apartment building at 4181 Madison, a house at 4171 Madison, and a house in the next block at 4148 La Salle Avenue. (The house at 4171 Madison was recently replaced by a larger structure).

Thomas Bros. Map reference: Page 42 at C 6.

At right, 4148 La Salle Avenue, Culver City.

The classic entrance to the old M-G-M studio complex.
at 10202 West Washington Boulevard, Culver City.

THE M-G-M SCHOOL

The M-G-M Schoolhouse.

Virtually every child actor employed by M-G-M during its golden years attended classes in this historic building on the old lot. Our Gang's kids studied there after 1938 when Metro began producing the series.

Thomas Bros. Map reference: Page 42 at C 6.

MAIN STREET, CULVER CITY

Because this street was used so many times in Laurel and Hardy and Our Gang films, I thought it would be appropriate to show it as it appears today.

Thomas Bros. Map reference: Page 42 at C 6.

A CULVER CITY LANDMARK

The Culver City Hotel, 9501 Culver Boulevard.

Thomas Bros. Map reference: Page 42 at C 6.

CULVER CITY/WEST LOS ANGELES

DIRECTIONS

The north border of the city of Culver City blends into West Los Angeles. A house seen in the Laurel and Hardy classic *SONS OF THE DESERT* (1) is in this area, located at 3725 Jasmine Avenue, north of Venice Boulevard. Nearby are many Our Gang locations.

Continue north on Jasmine Avenue to Tabor Street. Turn left (west) on Tabor Street and go to Motor Avenue. The building seen in the Our Gang film *BOUNCING BABIES* (2) is located on the northeast corner of the intersection. Its address is 3568/3570 Motor Avenue. Across Motor Avenue and slightly north was a house (3) also seen in the film. It was demolished recently. An office building now occupies the site. The address is 3545 Motor Avenue. Continue north on Motor Avenue. As you pass Woodbine Street and approach National Boulevard (4) you will be in the exact location the Our Gang fire truck and chief's car traveled en route to their first fire alarm in the film *HOOK AND LADDER*. Near the intersection of National Boulevard and Motor Avenue (on the east side of Motor Avenue) is the "Master Ornamental Iron and Electrical Welding Shop" (5) seen in the same film. The building is now occupied by an insurance agency. The address is 3316. Turn left (west) on National Boulevard. Old Engine Co. 43 (6) is located on the south side of National Boulevard. The address of the building is 10420. Return to Motor Avenue. Turn right (south) on Motor Avenue. Go to Woodbine Street. The building on the northeast corner at 3392 Motor Avenue (7) was seen in the Our Gang film *BOXING GLOVES*. Continue south to Tabor Street. Turn right (west) on Tabor Street and go to Overland Avenue. Turn left (south) on Overland Avenue. Three houses (8, 9 and 10) seen in the Our Gang film *FLY MY KITE* are on the left (east) side of Overland Avenue. The addresses are 3650, 3658 and 3668. On the opposite (west) side of Overland Avenue is the site of the field seen in the film. Apartment buildings now occupy the site.

Now to more Laurel and Hardy film locations. Go north on Overland Avenue from this site to National Boulevard. Turn right (east) and go to Motor Avenue. Continue east to Vinton Avenue. The site of the Laurel and Hardy film *BERTH MARKS* (12) is located north of National Boulevard, between Motor Avenue and Vinton Avenue. Return to Motor Avenue. Turn right (north) and follow Motor Avenue into Cheviot Hills. Turn left (west) on Ban-nockburn Drive and go to 10341. This house (13) is the one seen in the Laurel and Hardy film *BACON GRAB-BERS*. On the opposite side of the street, at the intersection of Bannockburn Drive and Haddington Drive, is the house (14) seen in the closing scenes of the same film. Its address is 2980 Haddington Drive.

Return to Motor Avenue. Turn left (north) and go to Dun-leer Drive. Turn right (east) and go to 10281 (15), the second house seen in Laurel and Hardy's *BIG BUSINESS*. Return to Motor Avenue. Turn right (north) and go to Club Drive. The houses on the east side of Motor Avenue at 2818/2826 (16) rest on the site of the house Laurel and Hardy built in one day in the film *THE FINISHING TOUCH*. The house across the street at 2817 (17) was also seen in the film.

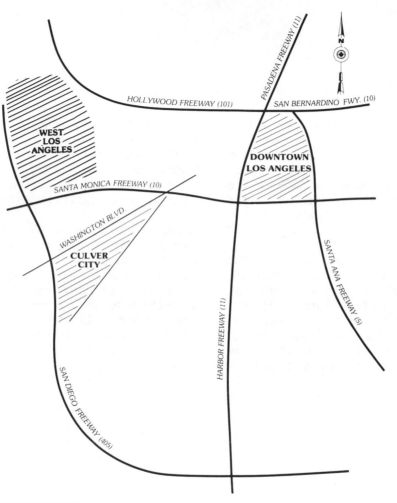

HOLLYWOOD FREEWAY (101)

PASADENA FREEWAY (11)

N

SAN BERNARDINO FWY. (10)

WEST LOS ANGELES

DOWNTOWN LOS ANGELES

SANTA MONICA FREEWAY (10)

WASHINGTON BLVD

CULVER CITY

SANTA ANA FREEWAY (5)

HARBOR FREEWAY (11)

SAN DIEGO FREEWAY (405)

MAP NOT TO SCALE

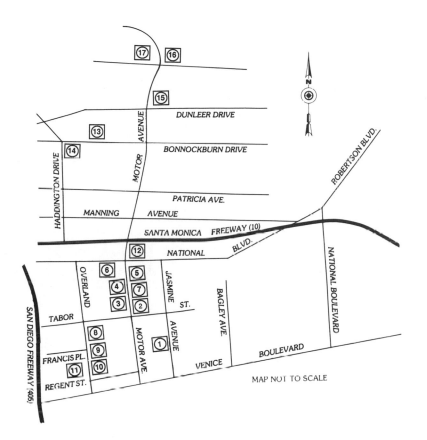

MAP NOT TO SCALE

SONS OF THE DESERT

THE PLAYERS

Stanley Laurel	Oliver Hardy	Charley Chase
Mae Busch	Dorothy Christie	Lucien Littlefield

Released December 29, 1933 by M-G-M

3725 Jasmine Avenue, Los Angeles.

In their most popular film, Laurel and Hardy sneak off to a convention in Chicago, telling wives Dorothy Christie and Mae Busch that the doctor has ordered a vacation in Hawaii. When the Boys come home, they are horrified to learn that the ship in which they were supposedly returning was sunk. They hide on the roof of their house during the memorable rain scene near the end of the film. After a hectic and hilarious reunion, the wives get a full confession.

The house has been razed and surrounding buildings are indistinguishable because the rooftop sequence was shot at night. Many experts placed the location at Clarington Avenue, north of Venice Boulevard, near Regent Street. After lengthy research, I discovered many daytime publicity stills of the rain scene. A house at 3725 Jasmine Avenue appears in several photographs and provides a point of reference that verifies the Clarington location.

Thomas Bros. Map reference: Page 42 at B 6.

BOUNCING BABIES

THE PLAYERS

Bobby "Wheezer" Hutchins

Jean Darling

Allen "Farina" Hoskins

Joe Cobb

Jackie Cooper

Norman "Chubby" Chaney

Mary Ann Jackson

Pete the Pup

Released October 12, 1929 by M-G-M

3568-3570 Motor Avenue, Los Angeles.

Wheezer (Bobby Hutchins), jealous of his newborn sibling, decides to return the baby to the hospital. His only problem is getting across an intersection. He tosses light bulbs onto the street; their ex-plosion stops the traffic. While drivers are checking their tires, Wheezer gets to the hospital—and into more trouble than he bargained for.

The busy intersection is at Motor Avenue and Tabor Street. The buildings seen in the film—3568/3570 Motor Avenue—were Bacon's Pharmacy and Safeway Stores, Inc. The buildings are now a cleaner/laundromat and supermarket. The buildings have changed little since the film was shot in 1929. The large structure seen in the distance (north) is the Palms School.

The stately old house seen many times in the background as Wheezer crossed Motor Avenue was at 3545 Motor. It has been replaced by an office building.

Thomas Bros. Map reference: Page 42 at B 6.

3545 Motor Avenue, Los Angeles, In 1984.

3545 Motor Avenue today.

Spanky and Dickie in fire chief's car on Motor Avenue.

HOOK AND LADDER

Motor Avenue, between Woodbine Street and National Blvd.

THE PLAYERS

George "Spanky" McFarland
Dorothy DeBorba
Pete the Pup

Matthew "Stymie" Beard
Dickie Moore

Sherwood "Spud" Bailey
Kendall "Breezy Brisbane" McComas
Dinah the Mule

Released August 27, 1932 by M-G-M

10420 National Boulevard, Los Angeles.

Our Gang members read a newspaper appeal for public cooperation with the fire department. They respond by converting a barn into their own private fire station, equipped with a horse-drawn engine and a chief's car. With these vehicles, they pay a visit to the real fire station—driving through Los Angeles streets that border Culver City—only to find that the firemen are some distance away answering an alarm.

On the way back to the barn, the Gang pass a building storing ex-plosives just as a fire breaks out. They pull the boxes of dynamite clear and manage to extinguish the flames, earning thanks and con-gratulations from the official fire fighters who finally arrive.

The building in the film was, indeed,

a real fire station: the home of Los Angeles City Engine Co. 43, located at 10420 National Boulevard. The big door at the left side of the building is now the window of a thrift shop. The big door on the building's right is now the entrance to a hair styling salon. The overall appearance of the building, including the tile roof, remains virtually unchanged over the decades.

The wide street where the Gang raced to the fire is Motor Avenue, between Woodbine Street and National Boulevard. A landmark seen near the end of their journey to the fire station was the Master Ornamental iron and Electric Welding Shop at 3316 Motor Avenue, just down the street from the fire station. The building, greatly altered, is now the home of an insurance company.

Thomas Bros. Map reference: Page 42 at B 5.

The old Master Ornamental Iron and Electrical Welding Shop.
3316 Motor Avenue.

Norman "Chubby" Chaney and Allen "Farina" Hoskins
in front of the building at Motor and Woodbine Avenue.

BOXING GLOVES

THE PLAYERS

Joe Cobb
Jackie Cooper
Jean Darling

Norman "Chubby" Chaney
Harry Spear

Allen "Farina" Hoskins
Mary Ann Jackson

Released September 9, 1929 by M-G-M

The intersection of Motor Avenue and Woodbine Avenue.

After fifty-nine years, the corner building seen in the opening segment of this Our Gang comedy still stands. It is now occupied by a plumbing contractor.

In the film, Joe Cobb and Norman "Chubby" Chaney continually bump into each other and drop bottles of soda pop on the sidewalk in front of this building as they rush to and from a nearby catering wagon in an attempt to impress cute little Jean Darling.

The location is 3392 Motor Avenue, at the intersection of Woodbine Street in Los Angeles.

Thomas Bros. Map reference: Page 42 at B 5.

Our Gang in the field. Note the houses in the background.

FLY MY KITE

3668 Overland Avenue.

THE PLAYERS

Allen "Farina" Hoskins	Mary Ann Jackson	Bobby "Wheezer" Hutchins
Margaret Mann	Norman "Chubby" Chaney	Matthew "Stymie" Beard
Dorothy DeBorba		Pete the Pup

Released May 30, 1931 by M-G-M

Grandma (Margaret Mann) is being evicted from her home by son-in-law James Mason. While packing, she comes across a stack of "worthless" bonds and gives them to the Gang for a kite tail. Mason, knowing that the bonds he hoped to acquire with the house are worth $100,000, is appalled to see them dangling from a kite in a nearby field. His attempts to retrieve the kite are, of course, foiled by the Gang.

Three of the houses, seen from the field near the end of the film, are on the east side of Overland Avenue—3650, 3658 and 3668—between Regent Street and Francis Place. They have changed little over the years, but are beginning to show their age. The large field where the Gang flew the kite was located on the west side of Overland Avenue, south of Francis Place. It is now occupied by many modern apartment buildings.

Thomas Bros. Map reference: Page 42 at B 6.

3650 Overland Avenue.

3658 Overland Avenue.

West side of Overland Avenue between Regent Street
and Francis Place.

Laurel & Hardy are tossed off the train at the "Pottsville" station, which in reality was the Palm Railway Station in Los Angeles.

BERTH MARKS

The spot where Stan and Ollie were tossed off
the train as it is today.

THE PLAYERS

Stanley Laurel   Oliver Hardy
Harry Bernard   Silas Wilcox
Baldwin Cooke   Pat Harmon   Charlie Hall

Released June 1, 1929 by M-G-M

Some Laurel and Hardy movie locations can be found with minimal effort. Others, however, take many hours of research - which were needed to verify the actual location of the final scene of this Hal Roach comedy filmed nearly six decades ago.

In the film, Stan and Ollie are en route by train to perform a musical act in Pottsville. As usual, they get involved in chaotic capers. When the train arrives in Pottsville, Ollie quickly learns that Stan forgot to take their musical instrument from the train, which is now long gone. Ollie then chases Stan down railroad tracks that curve from the Pottsville Station to the distant horizon, and throws a rock at him in anger.

The "Pottsville Railroad Station", at the time of filming, was the Palms Railroad Station. The building was constructed in 1887 and served the community until 1953 when it was sold to a private party. After abandonment and years of neglect, a grass roots movement to save it was formed in 1975 and it was moved to its present site in Heritage Square on February 12, 1976. The address of Heritage Square is 3800 N. Homer Street, Los Angeles.

I might add that Heritage Square, familiar to tens of thousands of

The original foundation of the "Pottsville" (Palms) station.

The Palms Railroad Station at Heritage Square.

visitors, does not qualify as an original movie location. Even though I had photographed the Palms Railroad Station in 1980, I did not include it in my previous publications, A GUIDE TO LAUREL AND HARDY MOVIE LOCATIONS (1982) and FOLLOWING THE COMEDY TRAIL (1984). Now, with the original site of the building authenticated, it indeed becomes a true part of Hollywood history.

The original cement foundation and the curved railroad tracks parallel the very busy Santa Monica Freeway and are behind a furniture manufacturing company that faces National Boulevard. Therefore, the only access is to follow the railroad tracks to the original site.

I find it easiest to approach from a point near the intersection of National Boulevard and Motor Avenue. A longer route is to approach from the opposite direction. To do this, begin near the intersection of Clarington Avenue and National Boulevard. The railroad tracks run behind a series of sign-boards on the north side of National Boulevard.

Whichever approach is made, when standing in front of the station site and looking to the west, one can easily imagine Stan running from Ollie in BERTH MARKS, and Carl "Alfalfa" Switzer of Our Gang stepping from the train, returning home on leave from military school to help George "Spanky" McFarland's football team beat a superior team headed by Dickie Jones in PIGSKIN PALOOKA (1937).

The site is south of the Santa Monica Freeway (10), north of National Boulevard, between Motor Avenue and Vinton Avenue in Los Angeles.

Palms Railroad Station.

Thomas Bros. Map reference: Page 42 at B 5.

The location where Ollie chased Stan at the end of the film.

In front of 10341 Bannockburn Drive.

BACON GRABBERS

10341 Bannockburn Drive, Los Angeles today.

THE PLAYERS

Stanley Laurel	Oliver Hardy	Edgar Kennedy
Jean Harlow	Charlie Hall	Bobby Dunn

Released October 19, 1929 by M-G-M

10341 Bannockburn Drive, Los Angeles today.

Having served Edgar Kennedy with a summons (see page 98), Laurel and Hardy are trying to repossess a radio that he bought on credit. At his Cheviot Hills home, they encounter predictable problems before achieving their goal.

"Kennedy's house", beautiful then and now, is at 10341 Bannockburn Drive. The intricate entryway as well as the two large windows of the second-story that face the street are featured in the film.

Another house, in the closing scene of the film, is across the street and at the end of the block. Its address is 2980 Haddington Drive.

Thomas Bros. Map reference: Page 42 at B 5.

2980 Haddington Drive, Los Angeles.

Fight in front of house at 10281 Dunleer Drive.

BIG BUSINESS

10281 Dunleer Drive, Los Angeles.

James Finlayson's house, the third and last stop on Laurel and Hardy's brief schedule, was some distance from their first stops in Culver City (see page 26). The house used in this segment of the film is in the Cheviot Hills section of Los Angeles. Its address is 10281 Dunleer Drive.

After nearly six decades, the only alterations visible from the street are a metal cover on the vent above the three windows on the right of the structure and two decorative cement blocks which now replace the eight-pane decorative window immediately to the left of the front door.

Thomas Bros. Map reference: Page 42 at B 4.

In front of the house at 2818/2826 Motor Avenue.

THE FINISHING TOUCH

THE PLAYERS

Stanley Laurel   Oliver Hardy
Edgar Kennedy   Sam Lufkin

Released February 25, 1928 by M-G-M

2818/2826 Motor Avenue.

Contractors Laurel and Hardy, in order to get a construction job, promise to finish the house in *one day*. As the building site is near a hospital, the noise soon draws the attention of a police officer (Edgar Kennedy). The Boys finish the house on time - but in typical Laurel and Hardy fashion, the house falls apart, the customer demands a refund, and the usual brawl ensues.

The correct location of this film site is 2818/2826 Motor Avenue, just north of Club Drive. The house across the street, often seen in the film, is at 2817 Motor.

NOTE: I stress the word correct because of an error in the original edition of FOLLOWING THE COMEDY TRAIL. Several fans insisted that the true location was some nine blocks north of the one I gave. They were so right and I was so wrong. Let me take this opportunity to apologize.

Thomas Bros. Map reference: Page 42 at B 4.

2817 Motor Avenue.

Stan and Ollie building the house with the house across
the street in the background.

WEST LOS ANGELES

VETERAN'S HOSPITAL GROUNDS

DIRECTIONS

Location # 1: Exit the San Diego Freeway (405) at Santa Monica Boulevard. Go west. Turn right (north) on Sawtelle Boulevard. At the intersection of Ohio Avenue and Sawtelle Boulevard is an entrance to the Veterans Hospital grounds. The plaque on the cement pillar was seen in the film *BLOCK-HEADS* (1938).

For Location # 2, continue north on Sawtelle Boulevard. The first road on the right is Dowlen Drive East. Follow it past the Veterans Hospital to the Wilshire Boulevard exit. On the left (west) is the site of the Old Soldiers Home used in the film. The grounds appear now much as they did in the film. DO NOT enter the grounds. Turn left (west) onto Wilshire Boulevard and turn left (south) at San Vicente Boulevard. Park and walk back across Wilshire. Look south across Wilshire to view the *BLOCK-HEADS* site.

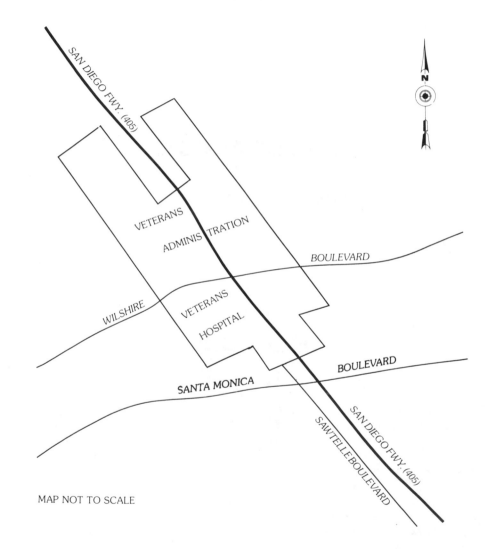

SAN DIEGO FWY. (405)

N

VETERANS

ADMINISTRATION

BOULEVARD

WILSHIRE

VETERANS

HOSPITAL

BOULEVARD

SANTA MONICA

SAWTELLE BOULEVARD

SAN DIEGO FWY. (405)

MAP NOT TO SCALE

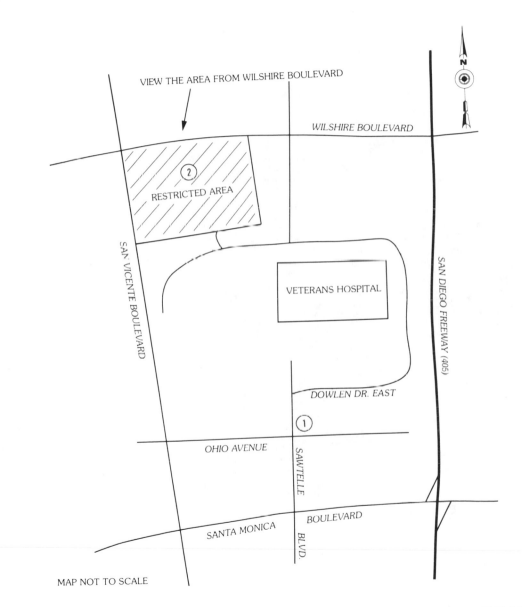

VIEW THE AREA FROM WILSHIRE BOULEVARD

WILSHIRE BOULEVARD

② RESTRICTED AREA

SAN VICENTE BOULEVARD

VETERANS HOSPITAL

SAN DIEGO FREEWAY (405)

DOWLEN DR. EAST

① OHIO AVENUE

SAWTELLE BLVD.

SANTA MONICA BOULEVARD

MAP NOT TO SCALE

N

BLOCK-HEADS

Sawtelle Boulevard and Ohio Street.

THE PLAYERS

Stanley Laurel	Oliver Hardy
Billy Gilbert	Patricia Ellis
James Finlayson	Minna Gombell
Harry Woods	Tommy Bond
Henry Hall	Sam Lufkin

Released August 19, 1938 by M-G-M

Oliver Hardy finds Stan Laurel in the Old Soldier's Home some twenty years after they parted on a battlefield in France during World War I. Hardy meets Laurel at the home and takes him to his apartment for a meal. Irritated by an unexpected guest, Mrs. Hardy (Minna Gombell) leaves in frustration. The Boys are left to cook for themselves and end up by creating havoc.

The reunion scene was filmed at the Old Soldier's Home, demolished years ago to make way for the Veterans Administration Hospital. The entrance to the area—marked by a plaque on a pillar—remains as it was in 1938. The location is at the intersection of Sawtelle Boulevard and Ohio Street.

The grounds seen near the Old Soldier's Home in the film are part of a private area of the VA complex. DO NOT ENTER THE GROUNDS. For a view, go to the intersection of San Vicente Boulevard and Wilshire Boulevard. The location of the film scene borders on the south side of Wilshire, east of San Vicente.

Both sites: Thomas Bros. Map reference: Page 41 at D 3.

Veterans Administration grounds.

SANTA MONICA

DIRECTIONS

Exit the Santa Monica Freeway (10) at Bundy Drive. Go south on Bundy Drive past the Santa Monica Airport. At National Boulevard, Bundy Drive becomes Centinela Avenue. The country road scene in the film is on the east side of Centinela Avenue just south of Airport Avenue.

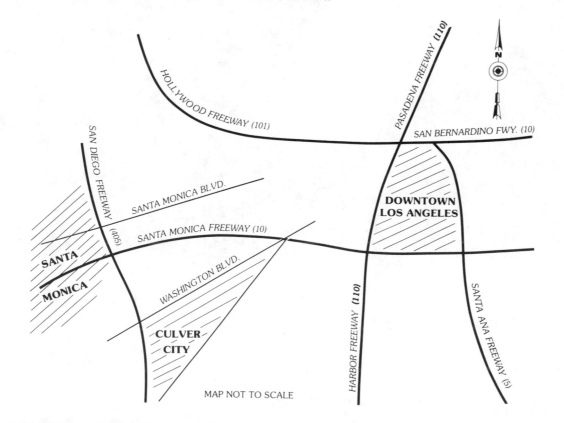

MAP NOT TO SCALE

N

SANTA MONICA FREEWAY (10)

BUNDY DR. (SOUTH)

OCEAN PARK BLVD.

SANTA MONICA
MUNICIPAL
AIRPORT

NATIONAL BLVD.

23RD STREET

CENTINELA AVENUE

(1)

AIRPORT AVENUE

MAP NOT TO SCALE

Traffic jam on Centinela Avenue in 1928.

TWO TARS

After leaving peaceful downtown Culver City (see page 42), Laurel and Hardy end up on a country road near the Santa Monica Airport. A traffic jam and Ollie's efforts to alleviate it lead to a pitched battle that destroys all the cars. The scene remains one of the all-time comedy classics in film history.

The location is on the east side of Centinela Avenue, south of the Santa Monica Airport.

Thomas Bros. Map reference: Page 49 at E 1.

The east side of Centinela Avenue, Los Angeles,

SOUTH CENTRAL LOS ANGELES

DIRECTIONS

Take the Harbor Freeway (110) to Slauson Avenue. Exit the freeway and travel west on Slauson Avenue to 2nd Avenue. For Location # 1 turn right (north) on 2nd Avenue and go to 4905. This beautiful house is seen in the closing segments of Laurel and Hardy's *COUNTY HOSPITAL.*

Continue north on 2nd Avenue for Location # 2. At the intersection of 48th Street is the building used in the same scenes. Its address is 4805.

Location # 3 is on the north side of 48th Street, west of 2nd Avenue: a row of buildings from the film.

Location # 4: Continue north on 2nd Avenue to Vernon Avenue. Turn right (east) on Vernon Avenue and go to Figueroa Street. Turn left (north) and go to Jefferson Boulevard. Turn left (west) on Jefferson Boulevard and go the short distance to the beautiful landmark, the Shrine Auditorium. Park in that area. Cross Jefferson Boulevard. Enter the University of Southern California campus. The Education and Information Studies Library is on the north side of 4th Street where Hoover Street terminates. This building was seen in the closing segments of *HOG WILD.*

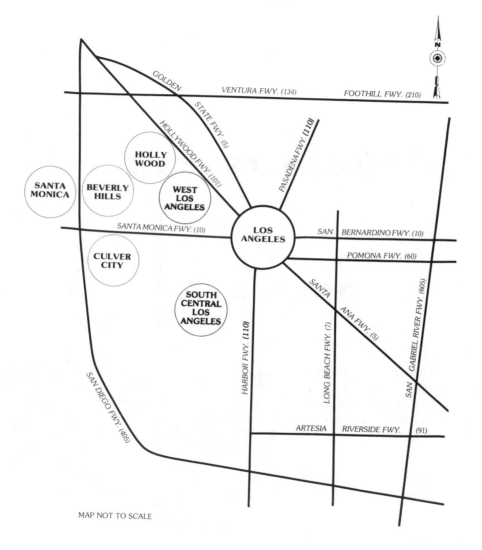

MAP NOT TO SCALE

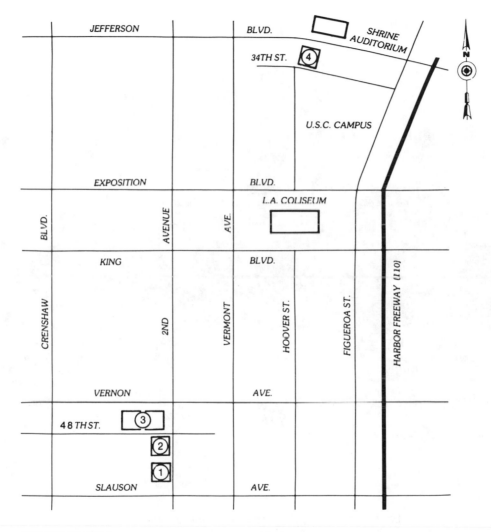

MAP NOT TO SCALE

Laurel and Hardy shortly before an accident with a
streetcar. House in background is virtually unchanged over five decades later.

COUNTY HOSPITAL

The house at 4905 2nd Avenue, Los Angeles.

The erratic car ride that began at the Culver City City Hall (see page 59) ends in a residential Los Angeles neighborhood many miles away, where Laurel and Hardy's Model T collides with a streetcar.

The house seen in this segment of the film, at 4905 2nd Avenue, is virtually unchanged today. A row of buildings in the sequence just before the accident are on the north side of

48th Street between 2nd and 3rd Avenues. Most of these buildings have been greatly altered, but a few still retain a bit of the 1930s charm.

The large building where the accident took place is located at 4805 2nd Avenue.

Thomas Bros. Map reference: Page 51 at D 3.

4805 2nd Avenue, Los Angeles.

The north side of 48th Street, between 2nd Avenue and 3rd Avenue, Los Angeles.

These stores appear directly behind the traffic officer (Sam Lufkin) near the end of the film

A wreck on the USC campus.

HOG WILD

The Education and Information Studies Library on the
University of Southern California campus at 34th Street
and Hoover Street, Los Angeles.

The wild car ride that begins in a Culver City residential neighborhood, ends after an accident with a street car on the University of California campus in the street next to the Education and Information Studies Library at 34th Street and Hoover Street in Los Angeles.

The arched windows and the decorative cornice that edges the roof of the library building absolutely verifies this building as the one seen in the closing scenes of the film.

As no streetcar tracks exist on Hoover Street today, I sought to verify if indeed they did exist in the past. A January, 1903 railway map substantiates that a north and south rail existed. Oddly, the street names were changed during the 20s and 30s as 35th Street became 34th Street, 37th Street became 35th Street and nearby Santa Monica Avenue became Exposition Boulevard.

Thomas Bros. Map reference: Page 44 at A 6.

Hoover Street looking south from the library building
(the approximate location of the street car wreck).

DOWNTOWN LOS ANGELES

DIRECTIONS

Exit any of the many freeways that border the downtown section of Los Angeles.

I suggest you begin at the "skyscraper"—Location # 1—seen in Laurel and Hardy's *LIBERTY*. The building is at 939 S. Broadway, on the northwest corner of Olympic Boulevard and Broadway. (Broadway is the seventh major street east of the Harbor Freeway (110).

The church, Location # 2, was at 1200 S. Los Angeles Street, on the southeast corner of the intersection of 12th Street and Los Angeles Street. From the skyscraper, continue south on Broadway to 12th Street. Turn left (west) on 12th Street and go two blocks to Los Angeles Street.

For Location # 3, continue south on Los Angeles to Washington Boulevard. Turn left (east) on Washington. Just beyond Santa Fe Avenue to the railroad tracks (west of the Los Angeles River), on the left (north) side of Washington, is the roundhouse seen in Our Gang's *RAILROADIN'*.

Location # 4: Return to Santa Fe Avenue. Turn right (north) and go to Porter Street. Turn right (east) and stop at the end of Porter Street at the railroad yards. Joe Cobb drove the *RAILROADIN'* locomotive under the bridge between Porter and Olympic Boulevard.

Location # 5, on the east side of the Los Angeles River, can be seen in the distance from Location # 4. It is the Sears Building, which appears many times throughout *RAILROADIN'*.

Return to Santa Fe Avenue for Location # 6. Turn right (north) on Santa Fe Avenue and go to the 4th Street Viaduct. Do not go under the viaduct. To your right (east) is an excellent view of the viaduct - the "bridge" seen behind the railroad car in which Mary Ann Jackson and other Gang members are riding in the opening scenes.

Location # 7: Continue north on Santa Fe Avenue to the 1st Street Viaduct, the location of the opening scenes of both *CHOO-CHOO!* (Our Gang) and *BERTH MARKS* (Laurel and Hardy).

To reach Location # 8, go farther north on Santa Fe Avenue, then turn left (west) on 1st Street. This roadway parallels the north side of the 1st Street Viaduct. Turn left at the termination of 1st Street and enter the viaduct. Cross the viaduct (east) and go to St. Louis Street. Turn right (south) and go to 4th Street. Hollenbeck Park and Hollenbeck Lake are on the right side of St. Louis Street. The lake is the site of the Laurel and Hardy film *MEN O' WAR*.

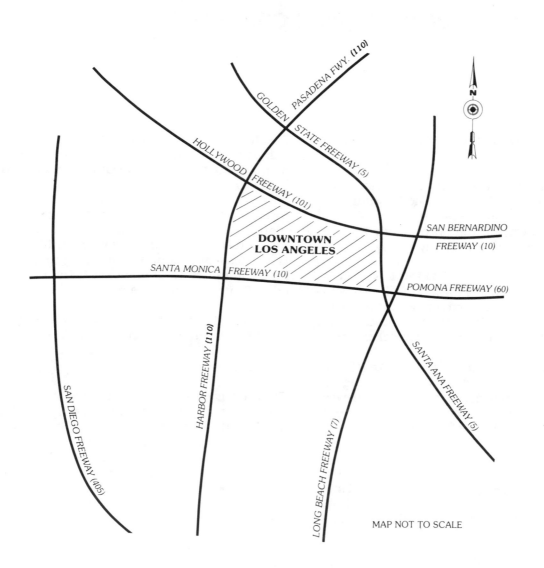

DOWNTOWN
LOS ANGELES

PASADENA FWY. **(110)**

GOLDEN STATE FREEWAY (5)

HOLLYWOOD FREEWAY (101)

SAN BERNARDINO FREEWAY (10)

SANTA MONICA FREEWAY (10)

POMONA FREEWAY (60)

HARBOR FREEWAY **(110)**

SAN DIEGO FREEWAY (405)

LONG BEACH FREEWAY (7)

SANTA ANA FREEWAY (5)

N

MAP NOT TO SCALE

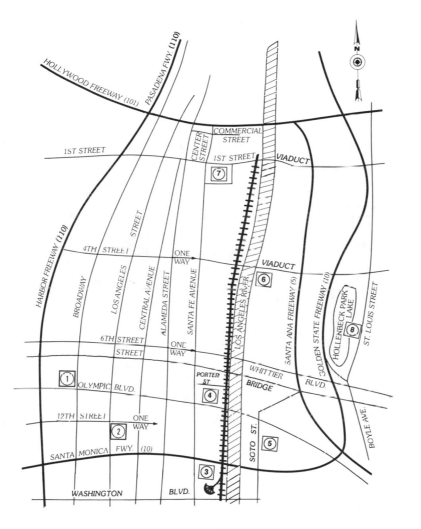

MAP NOT TO SCALE

LIBERTY

View of church and other buildings from roof
of 939 S. Broadway.

Laurel and Hardy escape from prison (see page 33) and end up in downtown Los Angeles at the top of a skyscraper under construction. It is here they finally get away from the policeman and go on their merry way.

The skyscraper is located at 939 S. Broadway. The above photograph was taken from the top of the building—the film site—facing south. The "V" intersection is Broadway Place cutting at an angle from Main Street (left) to Broadway (right). The church

The Boys on the top floor of the skyscraper with the
church and buildings in the background.

seen in the background appears in the final scenes of the film. The iron framework on top of the distant building is clearly seen in both the film and still photographs from 1929.

The lower-right photograph of the skyscraper was taken at the intersection of Broadway and Olympic Boulevard, looking north. The lower-left photograph shows the Broadway entrance to the building.

The LIBERTY Church (St. Joseph's Church, erected in 1901) was located at 1200 S. Los Angeles Street. I stress *was* as this beautiful building, sadly, was gutted by fire and subsequently demolished. A much smaller St. Joseph's Church was recently dedicated. It was constructed on the site of the original church seen in the film The church as it was will live on in the memory of Laurel and Hardy fans, through this film and the photographs on these pages.

Both sites: Thomas Bros. Map reference: Page 44 at C 4.

939 S. Broadway

Site of St. Joseph's Church in 1984 after the fire.

The new church built on the site seen in the film.

The triangle intersection of Main Street (left),
Broadway Place and Broadway (right).

The Boys looking down on the intersection.

RAILROADIN'

Santa Fe railroad yard roundhouse.

THE PLAYERS

Allen "Farina" Hoskins	Bobby "Wheezer" Hutchins	Jean Darling
Harry Spear	Joe Cobb	Mary Ann Jackson
Norman "Chubby" Chaney		Pete the Pup

Released June 15, 1929 by M-G-M

Our Gang goes to the railroad yards to see Joe (Joe Cobb) and Chubby's (Norman Chaney) dad (Otto Fries) who is an engineer. The plot of the film centers on a dream sequence wherein Farina (Allen Hoskins) fancies the Gang involved with a runaway train.

The roundhouse in the opening sequences was shot in the Santa Fe railroad yards, north of Washington Boulevard and east of Santa Fe Avenue. The large building seen in the film is the Sears Building, at 2675 E. 12th Street. The arched bridge Joe drives the locomotive under many times is the Olympic Boulevard Bridge. An excellent view of this bridge and the Sears Building is from the end of Porter Street, at the railroad tracks. The bridge seen behind the flatcar containing Mary Ann Jackson and other Gang members is the 4th Street Viaduct.

The Olympic Boulevard bridge was dedicated in 1925 in the memory of Caspar De Portola, the first governor of the state of California. The 4th Street Viaduct, under construction during the filming of this comedy, was dedicated in 1930.

As an item of interest, the railroad yards seen in this film parallel the Los Angeles River. This river is the primary reason the Pueblo of Los Angeles was founded near Sunset

Sante Fe railroad yard turntable.

The Olympic Boulevard bridge.

Boulevard and Alameda Street. Once the primary water source for Indians, settlers and the animals of the area, the river now is generally dry and serves a purpose only when the winter rains come to the area. Historically, it is the only river in the United States whose course was established by a city ordinance.

Thomas Bros. Map reference: Page 44 at F 6.

The 4th Street Viaduct.

The Sears Building, 2675 East 12th Street, Los Angeles.

Laurel and Hardy at the railroad station. Note 1st
Street Viaduct in the distance.

BERTH MARKS

300 Santa Fe Avenue, Los Angeles. Site of the old
Santa Fe Railroad Station.

THE PLAYERS

Stanley Laurel   Oliver Hardy
Harry Bernard   Silas Wilcox
Baldwin Cooke   Pat Harmon   Charlie Hall

Released June 1, 1929 by M-G-M

Laurel and Hardy are struggling musicians traveling by train from Los Angeles to Pottsville for an engagement. Sharing an upper berth makes sleep impossible. The trip is faster than they expected, and after making a quick exit, the Boys realize they are still in their under-clothes—and minus their musical instruments.

The site of the old Santa Fe Railroad Station is at 300 Santa Fe Avenue, immediately south of the 1st Street Viaduct, the bridge seen in the opening segment of the film.

The viaduct was completed in December of 1929, shortly before the film began production.

This site was also used for the opening segment of Our Gang's CHOO-CHOO! (see next page) three years later.

Thomas Bros. Map reference: Page 44 at E 3.

CHOO-CHOO!

The 1st Street Viaduct, 1st Street and Santa Fe Avenue,
Los Angeles.

THE PLAYERS

George "Spanky" McFarland
Kendall "Breezy Brisbane" McComas
Bobby "Wheezer" Hutchins
Dorothy DeBorba
Matthew "Stymie" Beard
Donald Haines
Sherwood "Spud" Bailey
Pete the Pup

Released May 7, 1932 by M-G-M

Hanging around the same railroad yards as seen in RAILROADIN' (see page 138), but a little farther north of the roundhouse, Our Gang members meet a group of children who have sneaked away from a train stopped at a nearby station en route to an orphanage in a distant city. The Gang and the orphans exchange clothing and the Gang boards the train for a hectic ride, the result of animals escaping from a freight car and exploding fireworks from the suitcase of a novelty salesman (Otto Fries).

The film site was near the 1st Street Viaduct. Its distinctive stairs provided the backdrop for the opening segment. The park where the Gang frolics as the train approaches and where they later exchange clothing with the orphans was the rest area of the old Santa Fe Railroad Station. The area is now occupied by a large building bordering the south side of the viaduct and looking west toward the Los Angeles River.

Thomas Bros. Map reference: Page 44 at E 3.

Hollenbeck Lake in 1929.

MEN O' WAR

Hollenbeck Park, on St. Louis Street between 4th Street and Hollenbeck Drive, Los Angeles.

THE PLAYERS

Stanley Laurel
James Finlayson
Anne Cornwall
Charlie Hall

Oliver Hardy
Harry Bernard
Gloria Greer
Baldwin Cooke

Released June 29, 1929 by M-G-M

Two sailors (Laurel and Hardy) are on shore leave. They find a lovely park with a huge lake—and two pretty girls to share the day. The Boys rent a boat and take the girls rowing. The pandemonium that follows includes the famous pillow fight.

The primary filming was in Hollenbeck Park, on St. Louis Street be-tween 4th Street and Hollenbeck Drive in East Los Angeles.

Major remodeling of the park (to make way for a freeway) greatly altered its west side and the lake. The stone-and-tile structure in the left photograph, however, remains unchanged. It can be seen in the film and in still photographs taken during filming. The beautiful arched wooden bridge was demolished during remodeling and replaced by a much smaller structure. The new bridge is at the west end of the lake in the right photograph.

Thomas Bros. Map reference: Page 44 at F 4.

THE SILVER LAKE AREA

DIRECTIONS

Exit the Hollywood Freeway (101) at Silver Lake Boulevard. Go north to Marathon Street. Turn left (west) and go to Descanso Drive (a circular street). Turn right.

Location # 1 is at 3278 Descanso Drive. This house was seen in Laurel and Hardy's *HATS OFF*.

Location # 2—the famous cement stairway just north of Location # 1—was seen in both *HATS OFF* and *THE MUSIC BOX*.

For Location # 3, continue down Descanso Drive a short distance to 3268. This is the famous "Stilt House" seen in *THE MUSIC BOX*.

Locations 4 and 5: Follow Descanso Drive north to Sunset Boulevard. Turn right (east) on Sunset Boulevard and go to Vendome Street. Turn right (south) and go to the intersection of Vendome and Del Monte. You are now at the foot of the stairway. It is located between 923 and 935 Vendome Street and was seen in both *HATS OFF* and *THE MUSIC BOX*.

Location # 6, across Vendome Street at the northeast intersection, is the duplex also seen in both films - 934 Vendome and 3025 Del Monte.

SUNSET BLVD.

DESCANSO DRIVE

DEL MONTE DRIVE

VENDOME STREET

RENO ST.

ROBINSON STREET

MARATHON STREET

SILVER LAKE BLVD.

HOLLYWOOD FREEWAY (101)

N

MAP NOT TO SCALE

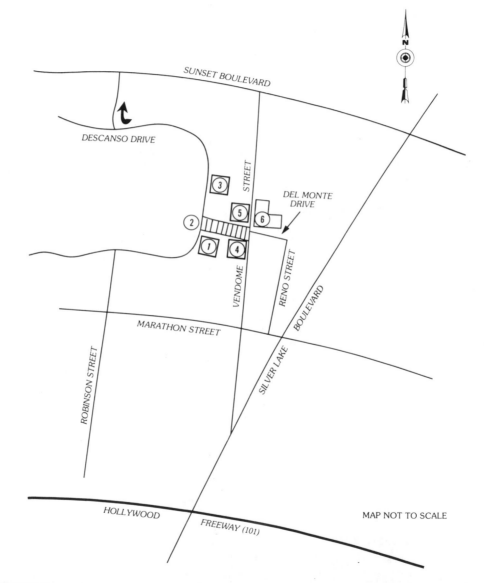

SUNSET BOULEVARD

DESCANSO DRIVE

N

STREET

③

⑤ ⑥

DEL MONTE
DRIVE

② ▦▦▦▦

① ④

VENDOME

RENO STREET

BOULEVARD

MARATHON STREET

ROBINSON STREET

SILVER LAKE

HOLLYWOOD

FREEWAY (101)

MAP NOT TO SCALE

HATS OFF

3278 Descanso Drive, Los Angeles.

The corner duplex apartment
building at 934 Vendome Street/
3025 Del Monte Drive, Los Angeles.

Deliverymen Laurel and Hardy are trying to heft a large laundry machine up a long flight of cement stairs. The struggle begins at Vendome Street and Del Monte Drive, the foot of the same stairs used in the Boys' Academy Award-winning THE MUSIC BOX (see Page 154).

Their goal is a house at the top of the stairs, 3278 Descanso Drive. The corner duplex, 934 Vendome/3025 Del Monte, seen in this film, is also prominent in THE MUSIC BOX.

Stan and Ollie end up tumbling down the stairway to an intersection, precipitating the famous street fight in which irate pedestrians destroy one another's hats (see page 45).

Note: On April 21, 1982 the Los Angeles Cultural Heritage Board considered designating the stairway a cultural-heritage location. The proposal was shelved. It will be reconsidered at a later date.

Thomas Bros. Map reference: Page 35 at B 5.

Looking down the stairs toward Vendome Street
from the sidewalk next to 3278 Descanso Drive.

The famous stairs.

THE MUSIC BOX

The stairs between 923 (left) and 935 (right)
Vendome Street, Los Angeles.

THE PLAYERS

Stanley Laurel		Oliver Hardy
Billy Gilbert	Charlie Hall	Gladys Gale
Sam Lufkin	Lilyan Irene	William Gillespie

Released April 16, 1932 by M-G-M

Laurel and Hardy are delivering a piano, a surprise gift from wife (Gladys Gale) to husband (Billy Gilbert). Stan and Ollie ask a neighborhood postman (Charlie Hall) for directions and learn that the house they seek is at the top of a long flight of cement stairs. After a monumental struggle, the Boys finally deliver the piano and are met by an irate Billy Gilbert. He hates pianos and with axe in hand, destroys this one.

The Boys on their delivery cart. Entrance to the corner
duplex at 3025 Del Monte Drive (in background) is virtually unchanged today.

The world famous stairs as the Boys prepare to
take a piano to the top.

The stairway is located between 923 and 935 Vendome Street. A duplex seen in the film when Laurel and Hardy arrive and unload the piano is located across the street from the stairway at 934 Vendome Street/3025 Del Monte Drive. The Stilt House seen in the middle of the film is located at 3268 Descanso Drive, at the top of the stairs.

The stairway itself has changed little over the decades. However, to the disappointment of Laurel and Hardy fans, the City of Los Angeles has installed light poles and a handrail on the stairway.

The building at 935 Vendome Street has changed little since filming except that the garage has a different door and the small window on its side facing the stairway has been boarded up and painted to match the stucco.

Many fans have asked for the exact number of steps that comprise the famous MUSIC BOX stairs. The answer is 131.

Thomas Bros. Map reference: Page 35 at B 5.

At the foot of the stairs, 935 Vendome Street, Los Angeles.

934 Vendome Street
Los Angeles.

3025 Del Monte Drive,
Los Angeles.

268 Descanso Drive, Los Angeles,
the "stilt" house.

HOLLYWOOD

THE WILSHIRE COUNTRY CLUB

DIRECTIONS

Exit the Hollywood Freeway (101) at either Hollywood Boulevard, Sunset Boulevard or Melrose Avenue. Travel west to Vine Street and turn left (south). After passing Melrose Avenue, Vine becomes Rossmore Avenue. Continue on to Rosewood Avenue. Turn right (west). This is the north side of the Wilshire Country Club. Stop at the intersection of Cahuenga Boulevard and Rosewood. The area south of Rosewood Avenue (the long line of eucalyptus trees) was the film site.

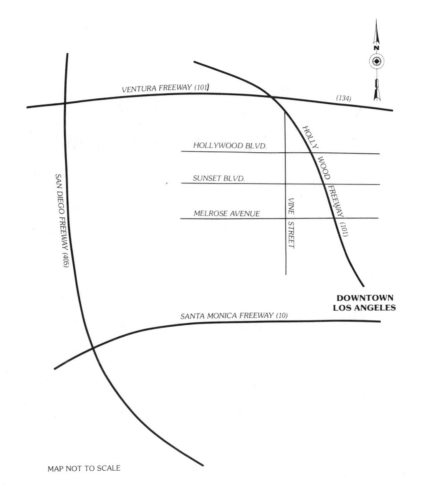

N

VENTURA FREEWAY (101)

(134)

HOLLYWOOD FREEWAY (101)

HOLLYWOOD BLVD.

SUNSET BLVD.

MELROSE AVENUE

VINE STREET

SAN DIEGO FREEWAY (405)

DOWNTOWN
LOS ANGELES

SANTA MONICA FREEWAY (10)

MAP NOT TO SCALE

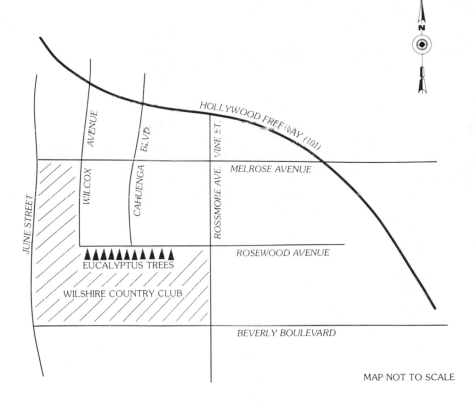

MAP NOT TO SCALE

The Boys digging a ditch in 1929.

THE HOOSE-GOW

301 North Rossmore, Los Angeles (the Wilshire Country Club).

THE PLAYERS

Stanley Laurel		Oliver Hardy
James Finlayson	Stanley Sandford	Dick Sutherland
Elinor Van Der Veer	Retta Palmer	Sam Lufkin

Released November 16, 1929 by M-G-M

Laurel and Hardy, on the wrong side of the law again, are sentenced to a prison camp. After botching assorted assignments, they are finally detailed to digging ditches with a road gang. When the governor of the state (James Finlayson) pays a visit, Laurel and Hardy get deeper into trouble by damaging his car.

The location of the prison camp was adjacent to the Wilshire Country Club at 301 N. Rossmore Avenue.

Members of the Hoose-gow company pinpointed the location at the west side of the country club property bordering Rosewood Avenue, west of Rossmore Avenue, where Cahuenga Boulevard ends. The row of eucalyptus trees at Cahuenga and Rosewood match those seen next to the ditch in the film and seem to verify the site.

Thomas Bros. Map reference: Page 34 at C 5.

BEVERLY HILLS

DIRECTIONS

Exit the San Diego Freeway (405) at Santa Monica Boulevard. Go east on Santa Monica Boulevard to Canon Drive. Turn left (north) on Canon Drive.

Location # 1, the curve of Canon nearing Carmelita Avenue, is the street seen in Laurel and Hardy's *BUSY BODIES*.

Location # 2: The Boys stopped in front of a house at 517 Canon Drive to change the record on a phonograph lo-cated under the hood of their Model T.

For Location # 3, continue north on Canon to the inter-section of Beverly Drive. The Will Rogers Memorial Park is the location of the opening scenes of the Laurel and Hardy film *PACK UP YOUR TROUBLES*.

The Beverly Hills Hotel, Location # 4, at 9641 West Sun-set Boulevard, was also seen in the film.

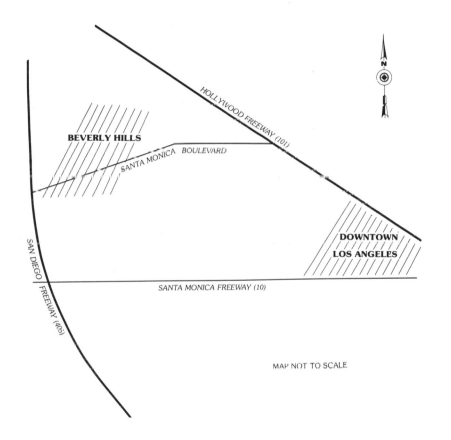

N

HOLLYWOOD FREEWAY (101)

BEVERLY HILLS

SANTA MONICA BOULEVARD

SAN DIEGO FREEWAY (405)

DOWNTOWN LOS ANGELES

SANTA MONICA FREEWAY (10)

MAP NOT TO SCALE

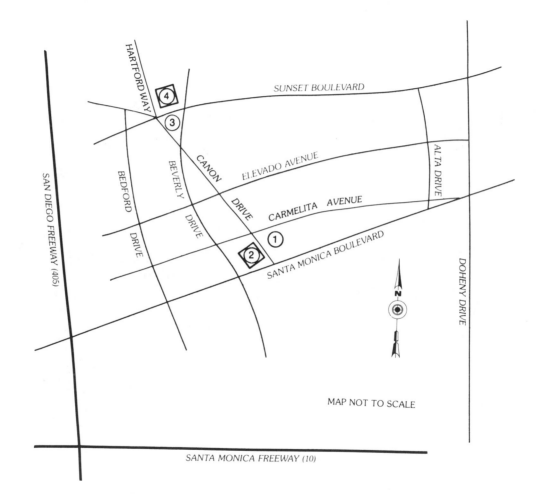

MAP NOT TO SCALE

BUSY BODIES

THE PLAYERS

Stanley Laurel   Oliver Hardy
Stanley (Tiny) Sandford   Charlie Hall

Released October 7, 1933 by M-G-M

Canon Drive, between Santa Monica Boulevard
and Carmelita Avenue, Beverly Hills.

Laurel and Hardy land a job at a lumberyard (actually the Hal Roach Studios). The film opens as they drive to work and closes as they drive through a sawmill, which cuts the Boys' Model T in half.

The opening scenes of the film were shot on Canyon Drive, between Santa Monica Boulevard and Carmelita Avenue in Beverly Hills. The distinctive rows of alternating date and Washingtonia palm trees lining Canon Drive are as prominent today as they were in the film. The

Laurel and Hardy and the Hal Roach crew during filming
on Canon Drive, near Carmelita Avenue.

Boys made one stop—at 517 North Canon Drive—to change a record on a phonograph machine concealed under the hood of their car. The house seen at this location can still be identified by the unique style of the front porch and the row of side windows that appear in the film segment.

Thomas Bros. Map reference: Page 33 at B 6.

517 North Canon Drive, Beverly Hills.

Learning of World War I while relaxing in the park.

PACK UP YOUR TROUBLES

THE PLAYERS

Stanley Laurel   Oliver Hardy   Tom Kennedy
Grady Sutton   Donald Dillaway   Jacquie Lyn

Released September 17, 1932, by M-G-M

Will Rogers Memorial Park, a beautiful 3-1/2 acre area, bounded
by Sunset Boulevard, Beverly Drive and Canon Drive.

This film opens with Laurel and Hardy sitting in a park reading a newspaper that reports the outbreak of World War I. Music in the distance heralds the approach of a recruiting sergeant (Tom Kennedy). The inevitable happens. While in boot camp, Laurel and Hardy befriend a soldier (Donald Dillaway) whose wife left him with a young daughter (Jacquie Lyn) to care for. At a battlefield in France weeks later, the Boys promise their buddy to take the child to her grandparents in case he doesn't return from battle. He doesn't. Back from the war, Laurel and Hardy begin a lengthy search for the soldier's parents. The big problem is that their surname is Smith. So where to begin? With the telephone book. Pages later, after a routine bank loan turns into an unintentional robbery, the Boys finally find Smith's parents and unite them with a granddaughter they have never seen.

The Will Rogers Memorial Park—a beautiful 3-1/2 acre area bounded by Sunset Boulevard, Beverly Drive and Canon Drive—was used in the opening scenes. The park still boasts many landmarks seen in the film. The walkway on which recruiting sergeant Tom Kennedy approached the Boys has changed little. Only a modern light post and drinking fountain have been added. The cement edge of the pond where Ted Kennedy tried to enlist a one-armed man is unchanged. Opened in 1915 as the Sunset Municipal Park, it's the oldest park in Beverly Hills. On July 8, 1952, it was renamed the Will Rogers Memorial Park in honor of the former mayor of Beverly Hills.

A Beverly Hills landmark, the Beverly Hills Hotel, was also used in the opening scenes. It is across the street from the park at 9641 West Sunset Boulevard.

Thomas Bros. Map reference: Page 33 at B 5.

The Beverly Hills Hotel, 9641 West Sunset Boulevard, Beverly Hills.

TOLUCA LAKE

DIRECTIONS

For easy access to this location, I suggest the Ventura Freeway (101) (134). If traveling west, exit at Hollywood Way. Turn left (west) on Alameda Avenue. Alameda Avenue joins Riverside Drive after a short distance. The next intersection after that juncture is Rose Street and Riverside Drive. Turn left (south) on Rose Street and continue to Lakeside Drive. There you will see the east shoreline of Toluca Lake. If traveling east on the Ventura Freeway, exit at Pass Avenue. Turn right (south) on Pass Avenue. Go to Alameda Avenue. Turn right (west) on Alameda Avenue, continue to Rose Street and follow the same directions to the lake.

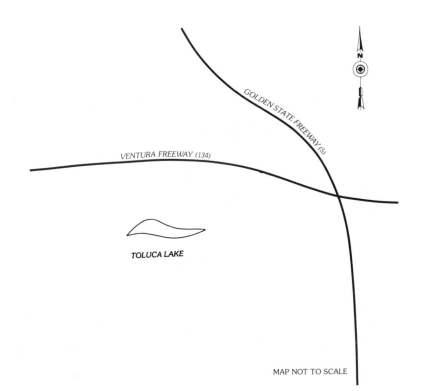

GOLDEN STATE FREEWAY (5)

N

VENTURA FREEWAY (134)

TOLUCA LAKE

MAP NOT TO SCALE

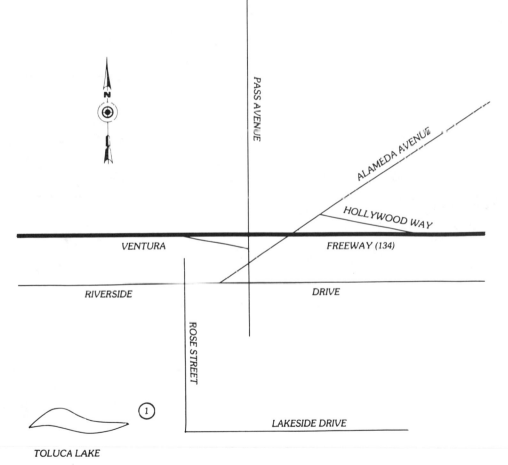

N

PASS AVENUE

ALAMEDA AVENUE

HOLLYWOOD WAY

VENTURA FREEWAY (134)

RIVERSIDE DRIVE

ROSE STREET

①

TOLUCA LAKE

LAKESIDE DRIVE

MAP NOT TO SCALE

Our Gang at Toluca Lake.

THREE MEN IN A TUB

THE PLAYERS

Carl "Alfalfa" Switzer
Darwood "Waldo" Kaye

Darla Hood
Billie "Buckwheat" Thomas

George "Spanky" McFarland
Eugene "Porky" Lee

Released March 26, 1938 by M-G-M

Toluca Lake.

Our Gang's Darla (Darla Hood) finds a new boyfriend (Darwood Kaye) who owns a nifty motorboat. Alfalfa (Carl Switzer), Darla's jilted boyfriend, becomes jealous, builds his own boat, then challenges Kay to a race that neither win because Kaye's boat sinks and Alfalfa stops his boat to rescue Darla.

Some scenes of this film were shot at Toluca Lake, a small but lovely body of water next to the Lakeside Golf Club of Hollywood at 4500 Lakeside Drive in Burbank.

The homes lining the lake have been altered significantly since 1938 and no distinctive landmarks exist to compare with scenes in the film.

Thomas Bros. Map reference: Page 24 at A 4.

Toluca Lake, next to the Lakeside Golf Club of Hollywood, 4500 Lakeside Drive, Burbank.

THEIR HOMES IN THE 1930's

DIRECTIONS

Exit the San Diego (405) Freeway at Santa Monica Boulevard. Go east to Bedford Drive and turn left (north).

Location # 1 is a beautiful house at 718 N. Bedford, the former home of Stanley Laurel.

Thomas Bros. Map reference: Page 33 at B 6.

For Location # 2, continue north on Bedford to Sunset Boulevard. Turn right (east) and go to Alta Drive. Turn right (south). At 621 Alta is the equally beautiful former home of Oliver Hardy.

Thomas Bros. Map reference: Page 33 at C 5.

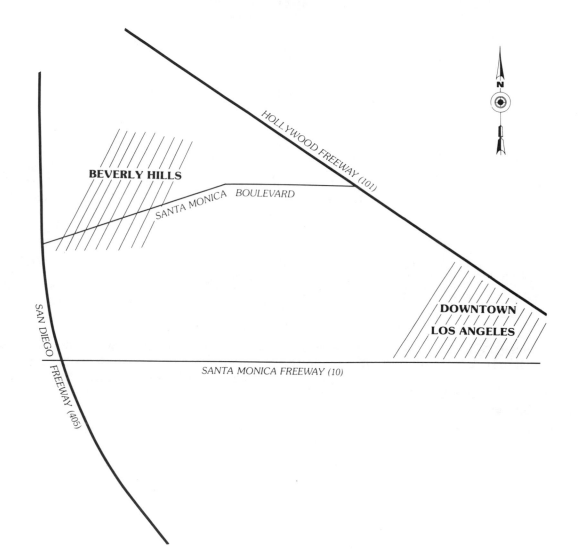

N

BEVERLY HILLS

HOLLYWOOD FREEWAY (101)

SANTA MONICA BOULEVARD

SAN DIEGO FREEWAY (405)

DOWNTOWN LOS ANGELES

SANTA MONICA FREEWAY (10)

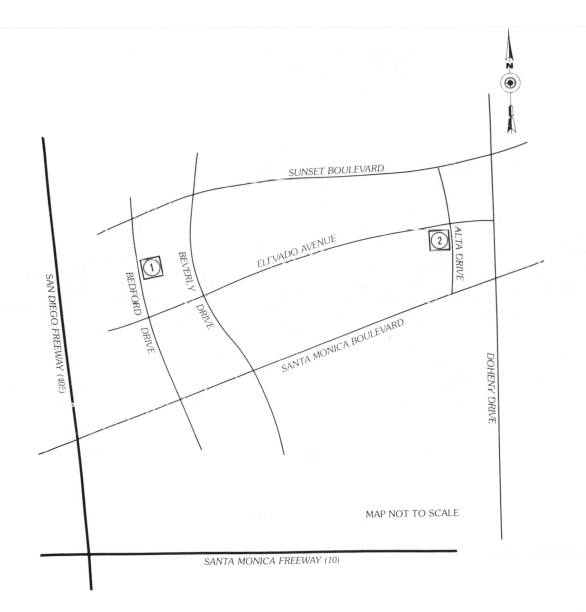

N

SUNSET BOULEVARD

ELEVADO AVENUE

SAN DIEGO FREEWAY (405)

BEDFORD DRIVE

BEVERLY DRIVE

① ②

ALTA DRIVE

SANTA MONICA BOULEVARD

DOHENY DRIVE

MAP NOT TO SCALE

SANTA MONICA FREEWAY (10)

718 North Bedford Drive, Beverly Hills, the former
home of Stanley Laurel.

621 Alta Drive, Beverly Hills, the former home
of Oliver Hardy.

A PLACE OF REST

STAN LAUREL

DIRECTIONS

Exit the Ventura Freeway (134) at Forest Lawn Drive. Travel west to the entrance of Forest Lawn - Hollywood Hills. Go south on Memorial Drive to Memory Lane. Turn left (east) and stop near the Monument to Washington.

Stanley Laurel's gravesite and plaque are behind the statue and slightly to the right (west).

Thomas Bros. Map reference: Page 24 at C 3.

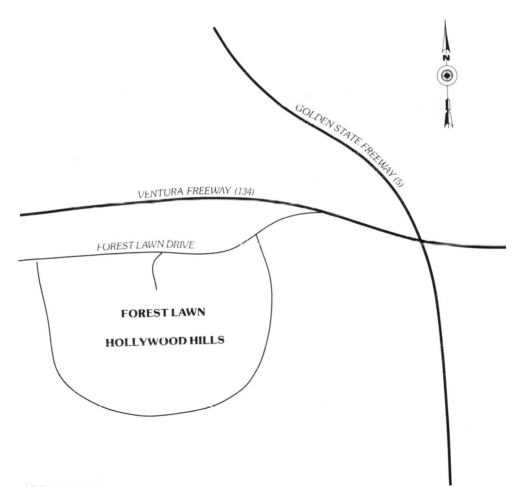

GOLDEN STATE FREEWAY (5)

N

VENTURA FREEWAY (134)

FOREST LAWN DRIVE

FOREST LAWN

HOLLYWOOD HILLS

MAP NOT TO SCALE

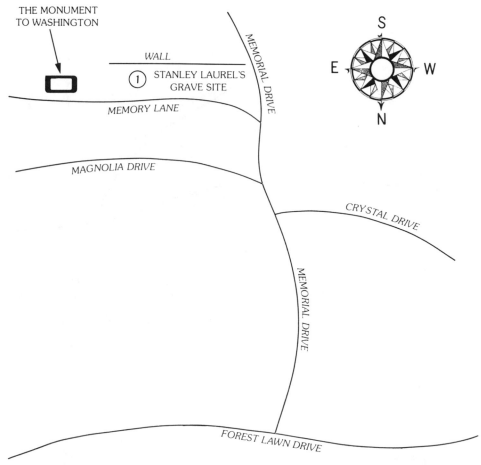

THE MONUMENT
TO WASHINGTON

WALL

① STANLEY LAUREL'S
GRAVE SITE

MEMORY LANE

MEMORIAL DRIVE

MAGNOLIA DRIVE

CRYSTAL DRIVE

MEMORIAL DRIVE

FOREST LAWN DRIVE

S

E   W

N

MAP NOT TO SCALE

STAN LAUREL

A PLACE OF REST

OLIVER HARDY

DIRECTIONS

Take the Hollywood Freeway (101) to Victory Boulevard. Go east on Victory Boulevard to 10621, the intersection of Cahuenga Boulevard. Turn left or right, depending on approach to the entrance of Valhalla Memorial Park. Keep to the right. Go north on the Avenue of Heroes three-tenths of a mile. You will pass the Mausoleum of the Good Shepherd and a small stone bench just west of a flagstone wall. The curb is marked "1069". On the east face of the wall is a plaque dedicated to Oliver Hardy by the Sons of the Desert, an international organization dedicated to perpetuating the comedic genius of Laurel and Hardy. A few steps east of the plaque is Ollie's final resting place.

Thomas Bros. Map reference: Page 16 at F 5

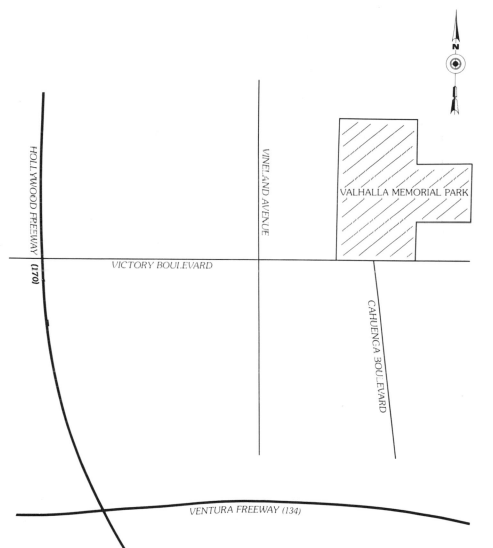

N

VALHALLA MEMORIAL PARK

HOLLYWOOD FREEWAY (170)

VINELAND AVENUE

VICTORY BOULEVARD

CAHUENGA BOULEVARD

VENTURA FREEWAY (134)

MAP NOT TO SCALE

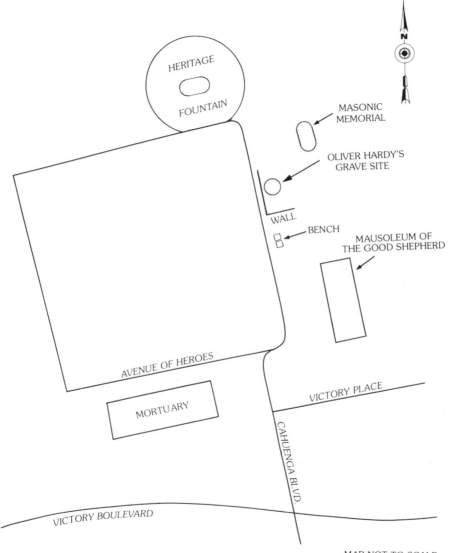

HERITAGE

FOUNTAIN

MASONIC
MEMORIAL

OLIVER HARDY'S
GRAVE SITE

N

WALL

BENCH

MAUSOLEUM OF
THE GOOD SHEPHERD

AVENUE OF HEROES

VICTORY PLACE

MORTUARY

CAHUENGA BLVD.

VICTORY BOULEVARD

MAP NOT TO SCALE

OLIVER HARDY

A PLACE OF REST

OUR GANG'S "ALFALFA" AND DARLA

DIRECTIONS

Exit the Hollywood Freeway (101) at Santa Monica Boulevard. Go west to 6000 Santa Monica, the entrance to Hollywood Memorial Park Cemetery. Turn left (south) and enter the grounds. Our Gang's Darla Hood and Carl "Alfalfa" Switzer are among the many Hollywood stars interred here. (A map of their gravesites is available in the office building at the left side of the cemetery entrance.) From the entrance, drive south to Maple Avenue. Turn left (east) on Woodlawn Avenue. Stop after approximately 50 yards. On the north side of Woodlawn Avenue, in Section 6, is the grave of Alfalfa (1). From this point, Darla's crypt is due west at the end of Woodlawn Avenue in the Abbey of the Psalms (2). The crypt is located in the Sanctuary of Light Wing on the 7th level in Section G-4 on the west wall. The number is 7213.

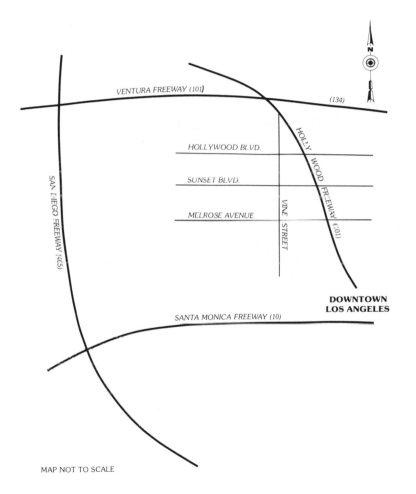

VENTURA FREEWAY (101)

(134)

HOLLYWOOD BLVD.

HOLLYWOOD FREEWAY (101)

SUNSET BLVD.

MELROSE AVENUE

VINE STREET

SAN DIEGO FREEWAY (405)

DOWNTOWN
LOS ANGELES

SANTA MONICA FREEWAY (10)

MAP NOT TO SCALE

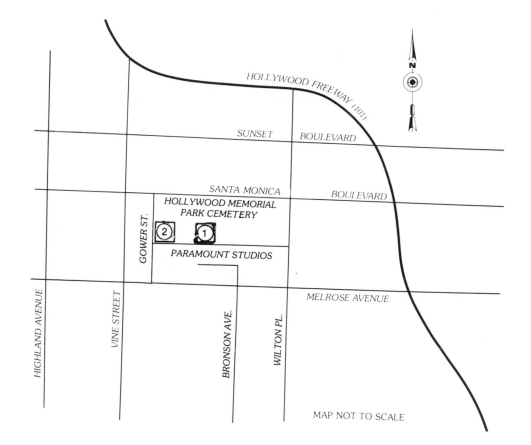

HOLLYWOOD FREEWAY (101)

N

SUNSET   BOULEVARD

SANTA MONICA   BOULEVARD

HOLLYWOOD MEMORIAL
PARK CEMETERY

GOWER ST.

② ①

PARAMOUNT STUDIOS

HIGHLAND AVENUE

VINE STREET

BRONSON AVE.

WILTON PL.

MELROSE AVENUE

MAP NOT TO SCALE

OUR GANG'S "ALFALFA" AND DARLA

Hollywood Memorial Park Cemetery, 6000 Santa Monica

Boulevard, Los Angeles.

North of Woodlawn Avenue in Section 6 lies Alfalfa.

Abbey of the Psalms.

Darla's crypt in the Sanctuary of Light wing
on the 7th level in Section G4, west wall.

A PLACE OF REST

OUR GANG'S "MISS CRABTREE" AND "PETE THE PUP"

My 1984 book, FOLLOWING THE COMEDY TRAIL, inspired many letters from Our Gang buffs. Most wanted locations of additional films—which I've listed in this book. They asked "Where are they now?" That has been extensively covered in the outstanding OUR GANG by Leonard Maltin and Richard W. Bann (Crown Publishers, 1977), which I highly recommend.

To fulfill numerous requests, I located the gravesite of June Marlowe, the lovely Miss Crabtree of early Our Gang talkies. I was fortunate enough to establish correspondence with June Marlowe during the latter years of her life. She not only graciously answered all my letters but sent a personally inscribed photograph of herself on a movie set. It holds a proud place on my office wall.

June Marlowe (Mrs. Rodney Sprigg) was buried in Mission Cemetery, 11160 Stranwood Avenue, north of San Fernando Mission Boulevard, west of the Golden Gate Freeway (5) and east of the San Diego Freeway (405) in Mission Hills.

A surprising number of letters requested the location of the grave of "Pete the Pup", who was definitely considered an actor—and, more important, a friend—by those associated with Our Gang over the years.

Pete rests near the top of a shady hill at the Los Angeles S.P.C.A. Pet Memorial Park, 5068 Old Scandia Lane, north of the Ventura Freeway (101) in Calabasas.

Thomas Bros. Map reference: Page 8 at C 1 (Miss Crabtree), Page 100 at D 3 (Pete the Pup).

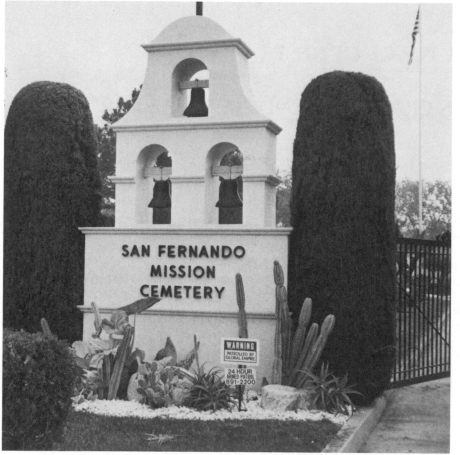

11160 Stranwood Avenue, Mission Hills.

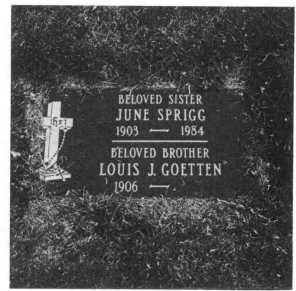

June Marlowe (Sprigg), the
beloved "Miss Crabtree".

5068 Old Scandia Lane, Calabasas.

Pete's grave.

"Our Gang" in the car with Miss Crabtree.

IN THEIR MEMORY

DIRECTIONS

From the Hollywood Freeway (101), turn west onto Hollywood Boulevard. Sidewalks in the downtown Hollywood area are imprinted with stars that commemorate the "greats"—actors, directors, producers, et al—of the film industry.

Location # 1, the Stanley Laurel star, is in front of 7021 Hollywood Boulevard, west of the Chinese Theatre.

Oliver Hardy's star - Location # 2—is on the northeast corner of the intersection of Sunset Boulevard and Vine Street (three stars north of Sunset on Vine).

Location # 3, the Home Savings and Loan building at 1500 N. Vine, as a point of interest, is the site of a mosaic. Laurel and Hardy's names are inscribed on the column left of the building's entrance.

Thomas Bros. Map reference: Page 34 at B 3 - Laurel star, Page 34 at C 3 - Hardy star and mosaic.

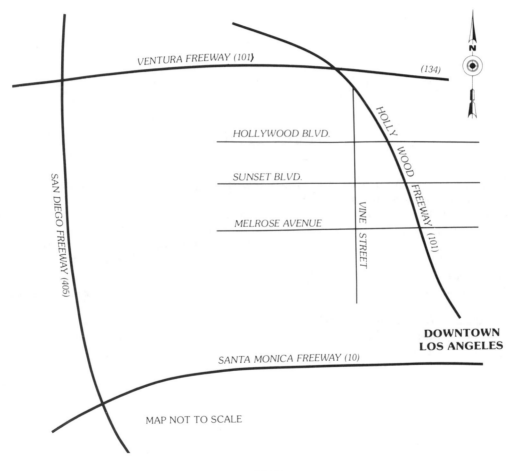

VENTURA FREEWAY (101)

(134)

N

HOLLYWOOD BLVD.

SUNSET BLVD.

MELROSE AVENUE

SAN DIEGO FREEWAY (405)

HOLLYWOOD FREEWAY (101)

VINE STREET

DOWNTOWN
LOS ANGELES

SANTA MONICA FREEWAY (10)

MAP NOT TO SCALE

MAP

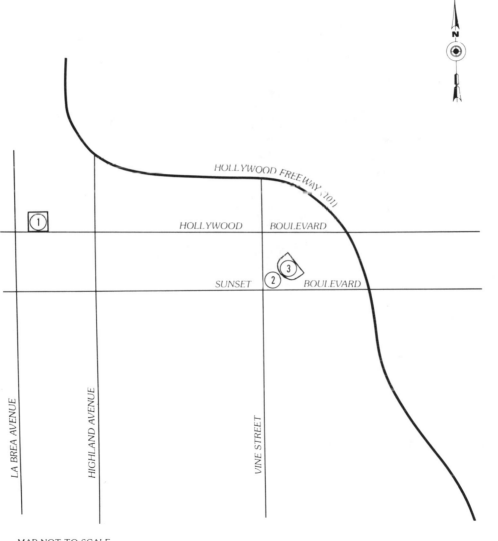

N

HOLLYWOOD FREEWAY (101)

HOLLYWOOD   BOULEVARD

①

SUNSET   BOULEVARD

② ③

LA BREA AVENUE

HIGHLAND AVENUE

VINE STREET

MAP NOT TO SCALE

HOLLYWOOD STARS

7021 Hollywood Boulevard, Hollywood.

1500 N. Vine Street, Hollywood.

LAUREL AND HARDY MOSAIC

The Boys are listed with other movie greats on the front of the Home Savings and Loan building (1500 N. Vine Street, Hollywood). Their names appear on the column bordering the left side of the entrance.

FOR YOUR INFORMATION

Good old Santa Fe engine # 1373 appears in RAILROADIN' (1929) and one year later in PUPS IS PUPS.

The massive prison set used by M-G-M in the epic THE BIG HOUSE in 1930 was also used by the Boys in their prison "epic" PARDON US the following year. The set was constructed on Lot #2. The lot was sold to private investors and is now a beautiful residential section of Culver City. The architects responsible for design and construction, thankfully, remembered many M-G-M stars. Rooney Ave., Tracy Circle, Lamarr Ave., and Garland Drive are just a few streets that crisscross the area. Lot #2, bounded by Overland Avenue, Washington Blvd., Culver Blvd. and Elenda Street, was located immediately west of the central studio complex.

A FINAL WORD

My goal continues to be the location and verification of all existing Laurel and Hardy and Our Gang movie sites to provide enjoyment to their countless fans who deem to pay homage to them either through publications such as this or in-person. Again, time and progress remain the greatest enemy. This, coupled with the so called "unknown" movie site locations, make the task of "discovery" at times extremely difficult. Thus, I would deeply appreciate hearing from anyone who might have a shred of evidence so yet another treasured movie location could be permanently recorded for all fans of Laurel and Hardy and Our Gang to enjoy.

Information may be sent to me at the Publisher's address.

Leon Smith
c/o Pomegranate Press, Ltd.
3236 Bennett Drive
Los Angeles, CA 90068